HOLY WEEK – VOLUME 2   +

THE SERVICES OF HOLY FRIDAY

Music arranged and edited by

David Drillock
Helen Breslich Erickson
John H. Erickson

English text

Orthodox Church in America
Holy Friday Matins (1980)
Vespers of Holy Friday (1982)

Manuscript and Technical Preparation
Vladimir J. Nehrebecki
Leonard Soroka
Constance J. Tarasar

ST. VLADIMIR'S SEMINARY PRESS
Crestwood, New York
1983

ISBN 0-913836-87-7 Paperbound
ISBN 0-913836-88-5 Hardbound
Copyright St. Vladimir's Seminary Press
1983

Table of Contents

MATINS

THE GREAT LITANY
Kievan Chant — B. Ledkovsky 7
S. Glagolev 7
Byzantine Chant 8
Russian Chant 9
Znamenny Chant — A. Arkhangelsky 9

ALLELUIA & TROPARION
Kievan Chant — Traditional 10
Kievan Chant — P. Turchaninov 13
Kievan Chant — D. Soloviev 17
Byzantine Chant 20

THE LITTLE LITANY
Russian Chant 22
Znamenny Chant — A. Arkhangelsky 22

AT THE GOSPEL
Kievan 23
Russian Chant 24
Byzantine Chant 25

ANTIPHON I
Obikhod — N. Bakhmetev 26

ANTIPHON II
Obikhod — N. Bakhmetev 28

ANTIPHON III
Obikhod — N. Bakhmetev 30

THE LITTLE LITANY
Russian Chant 35
Znamenny Chant — A. Arkhangelsky 35

KATHISMA HYMN
Obikhod — N. Bakhmetev 36
Carpatho-Russian 37

AT THE GOSPEL
Kievan 39

ANTIPHON IV
Obikhod — N. Bakhmetev 40

ANTIPHON V
Obikhod — N. Bakhmetev 44

ANTIPHON VI
Obikhod — N. Bakhmetev 46

THE LITTLE LITANY
Russian Chant 50
Znamenny Chant — A. Arkhangelsky 50

KATHISMA HYMN
Obikhod — N. Bakhmetev 51
Carpatho-Russian 52

ANTIPHON VII
Obikhod — N. Bakhmetev 55

ANTIPHON VIII
Obikhod — N. Bakhmetev 57

ANTIPHON IX
Obikhod — N. Bakhmetev 60

THE LITTLE LITANY
Russian Chant 63
Znamenny Chant — A. Arkhangelsky 63

KATHISMA HYMN
Obikhod — N. Bakhmetev 64
Carpatho-Russian 65

AT THE GOSPEL
Kievan 66

ANTIPHON X
Obikhod — N. Bakhmetev 67

ANTIPHON XI
Obikhod — N. Bakhmetev 69

ANTIPHON XII
Obikhod — N. Bakhmetev 73

THE LITTLE LITANY
Russian Chant 77
Znamenny Chant — A. Arkhangelsky 77

KATHISMA HYMN
Obikhod — N. Bakhmetev 78
Carpatho-Russian 79

AT THE GOSPEL
Kievan 80

ANTIPHON XIII
Obikhod — N. Bakhmetev 81

ANTIPHON XIV
Obikhod — N. Bakhmetev 83

ANTIPHON XV
Obikhod — N. Bakhmetev 85
Byzantine Chant 89

THE LITTLE LITANY
Russian Chant 92
Znamenny Chant — A. Arkhangelsky 92

KATHISMA HYMN
Obikhod — N. Bakhmetev 93
After Kastalsky 94

AT THE GOSPEL
Kievan 95

THE BEATITUDES — Verses 96

THE BEATITUDES
Carpatho-Russian 98
Russian Chant 102

THE LITTLE LITANY
Russian Chant 106
Znamenny Chant — A. Arkhangelsky 106

THE PROKEIMENON
Obikhod — N. Bakhmetev 107
Znamenny Chant — A. Arkhangelsky 107

AT THE GOSPEL
Kievan 108

PSALM 51 – Text 109

AT THE GOSPEL
Kievan 110

THE KANON — ODE 5
Znamenny Chant — Klimov-Lebedev 111
Znamenny Chant — P. Turchaninov 112

THE LITTLE LITANY
Russian Chant 114
Znamenny Chant — A. Arkhangelsky 114

THE KONTAKION
Obikhod — N. Bakhmetev 115
A. Kastalsky 116

THE KANON — ODE 8
Znamenny Chant — Klimov-Lebedev 117
Znamenny Chant — P. Turchaninov 118

THE KANON – ODE 9
Znamenny Chant – Klimov-Lebedev 121
Znamenny Chant – P. Turchaninov 122
THE EXAPOSTILARION: THE WISE THIEF
Kievo-Pecherskaya Lavra 124
H. Benigsen/J. Erickson 125
Staritsky 126
M. Lisitsin 127
Byzantine Chant 128
Kievan Chant – B. Ledkovsky 129
B. Ledkovsky 130
AT THE GOSPEL
Kievan 134
THE PRAISES – Text 135
THE PRAISES
Obikhod – N. Bakhmetev 136
A. Kastalsky 143
AT THE GOSPEL
Kievan 150
THE LESSER DOXOLOGY – Text 151
LITANY OF FERVENT SUPPLICATION
Kievan Chant – B. Ledkovsky 152
S. Glagolev 153
Russian Chant 154
Znamenny Chant – A. Arkhangelsky 155
AT THE GOSPEL
Kievan 156
THE APOSTIKHA
Obikhod – N. Bakhmetev 157
Kievan Chant – A. Kastalsky 166
AT THE GOSPEL
Kievan 174
THE TRISAGION PRAYERS – Text 175
THE TROPARION
D. Yaichkov 176
Kievan Chant 177
THE AUGMENTED LITANY
Kievan Chant – B. Ledkovsky 178
S. Glagolev 178
Russian Chant 179
Znamenny Chant – A. Arkhangelsky 179
Byzantine Chant 180
Kievan Chant 180
THE GREAT DISMISSAL
B. Ledkovsky 181

ROYAL HOURS

THE FIRST HOUR – Text 184
The Prokeimenon of the Prophecy
Znamenny Chant – A. Arkhangelsky 185
THE THIRD HOUR – Text 186
The Prokeimenon of the Prophecy
Znamenny Chant – A. Arkhangelsky 187
THE SIXTH HOUR – Text 188
The Prokeimenon of the Prophecy
Znamenny Chant – A. Arkhangelsky 189
THE NINTH HOUR – Text 190
The Prokeimenon of the Prophecy
Znamenny Chant – A. Arkhangelsky 191

VESPERS

THE GREAT LITANY
Kievan Chant – B. Ledkovsky 194
Carpatho-Russian 194
Byzantine Chant 195
Russian Chant 196
Znamenny Chant – A. Arkhangelsky 196
LORD, I CALL UPON THEE
Obikhod – N. Bakhmetev 197
Kievan Chant – B. Ledkovsky 211
O GLADSOME LIGHT
Abbrev. Kievan Chant–B. Ledkovsky 228
Kievan Chant – B. Ledkovsky 230
Greek Melody 232
Kievan Chant – Arch. Theofan 234
Byzantine Chant 236
THE FIRST PROKEIMENON
Obikhod – N. Bakhmetev 238
Znamenny Chant – A. Arkhangelsky 238
THE SECOND PROKEIMENON
Obikhod – N. Bakhmetev 239
Znamenny Chant – A. Arkhangelsky 239
THE THIRD PROKEIMENON
Obikhod – N. Bakhmetev 240
Znamenny Chant – A. Arkhangelsky 240
ALLELUIA BEFORE THE GOSPEL
Znamenny Chant – A. Arkhangelsky 241
Modern Greek 241
Abbreviated Kievan Chant 241
AT THE GOSPEL
Kievan 242
Byzantine Chant 243
Russian Chant 244
THE AUGMENTED LITANY
Kievan Chant – B. Ledkovsky 245
S. Glagolev 246
Znamenny Chant – A. Arkhangelsky 247
Russian Chant 248
VOUCHSAFE, O LORD – Text 248
LITANY OF FERVENT SUPPLICATION
Kievan Chant – B. Ledkovsky 249
Russian Chant 250
Znamenny Chant – A. Arkhangelsky 251
THE APOSTIKHA
Obikhod – N. Bakhmetev 252
Optino Monastery Chant, and 261
Pskov Chant – H. Benigsen 266
THE PRAYER OF ST. SIMEON – Text 269
THE TRISAGION PRAYERS – Text 269
THE NOBLE JOSEPH
Bulgarian Melody 270
Greek Melody 274
Serbian Melody 276
THE GREAT DISMISSAL
B. Ledkovsky 279
COME, LET US BLESS JOSEPH
Pskov Chant – H. Benigsen 281
D. Bortniansky 284

MATINS

The Great Litany

Kievan Chant
B. Ledkovsky

The Great Litany

S. Glagolev

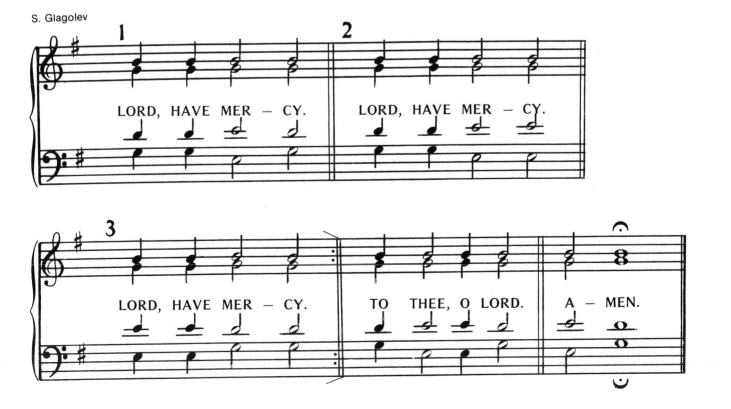

The Great Litany

Byzantine Chant

The Great Litany

Russian Chant

LORD, HAVE MER — CY. TO THEE, O LORD A — MEN.

The Great Litany

Znamenny Chant
A. Arkhangelsky

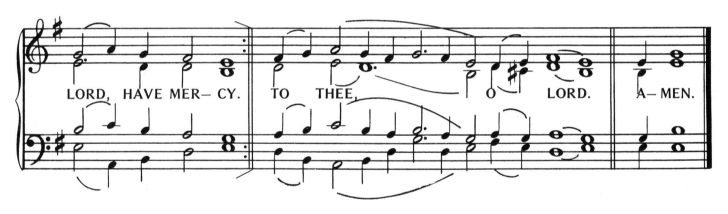

LORD, HAVE MER— CY. TO THEE, O LORD. A—MEN.

Alleluia

Kievan Chant
Traditional

Tone 8

AL–LE–LU — — IA, AL–LE–LU–IA, AL–LE–LU — — — — — — — — IA.

Verses:

In the night my soul rises early for Thee, O God, for Thy commandments are a light on the earth.
Alleluia (3 times)
Learn righteousness, you inhabitants of the earth.
Alleluia (3 times)
Jealousy shall grasp an untaught people.
Alleluia (3 times)
Bring more evils on them, O Lord, bring more evils on those who are glorious on the earth.

The Troparion

Kievan Chant
Traditional

Tone 8

WHEN THE GLOR — — I–OUS DISCIPLES WERE EN–LIGHT — — — — — — — — ENED

AT THE WASHING OF THEIR FEET BE–FORE THE SUP — — — — — — — — PER,

A—GAINST THE MAS — — — — — — TER. O LORD WHO ART

GOOD TOWARDS ALL MEN, GLO — — RY TO THEE!

GLO—RY TO THE FATHER, AND TO THE SON, AND TO THE HO—LY SPIR — IT.

Repeat: When the glorious disciples...

NOW AND EVER AND UNTO AGES OF A — GES. A — MEN.

Repeat: When the glorious disciples...

Alleluia

Kievan Chant
P. Turchaninov

Tone 8

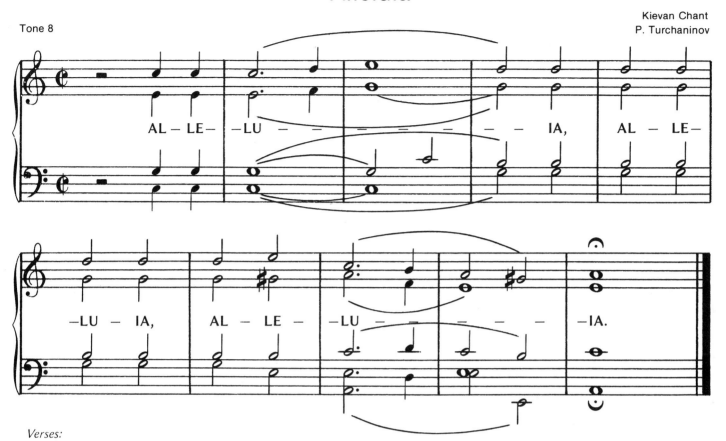

AL – LE– –LU – – – – – – – IA, AL – LE– –LU – IA, AL – LE – –LU – – – – – –IA.

Verses:

In the night my soul rises early for Thee, O God, for Thy commandments are a light on the earth.
Alleluia (3 times)
Learn righteousness, you inhabitants of the earth.
Alleluia (3 times)
Jealousy shall grasp an untaught people.
Alleluia (3 times)
Bring more evils on them, O Lord, bring more evils on those who are glorious on the earth.
Alleluia (3 times)

The Troparion

Kievan Chant
P. Turchaninov

Tone 8

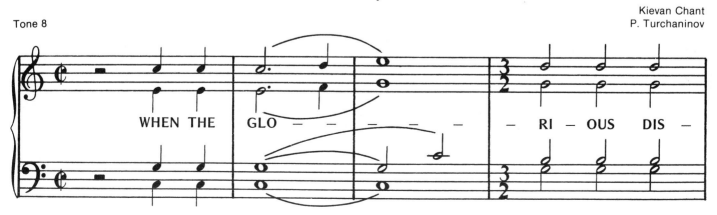

WHEN THE GLO – – – – – – RI – OUS DIS –

MAS — — — —TER O LORD WHO ART

GOOD TOWARDS ALL MEN GLO — —RY TO THEE.

GLO—RY TO THE FATHER, AND TO THE SON, AND TO THE HO—LY SPIR — IT.

Repeat: When the glorious disciples...

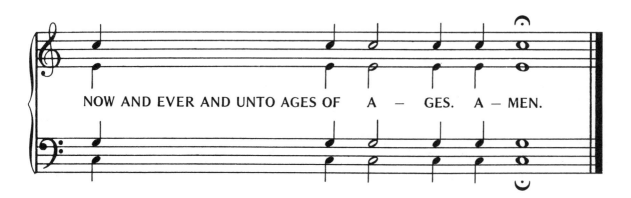

NOW AND EVER AND UNTO AGES OF A — GES. A — MEN.

Repeat: When the glorious disciples...

Alleluia

Tone 8
Women's Trio

Kievan Chant
D. Soloviev

AL–LE–LU — — IA, AL–LE–LU–IA, AL–LE–LU — — — IA.

Verses:

In the night my soul rises early for Thee, O God, for Thy commandments are a light on the earth.

Alleluia (3 times)

Learn righteousness, you inhabitants of the earth.

Alleluia (3 times)

Jealousy shall grasp an untaught people.

Alleluia (3 times)

Bring more evils on them, O Lord, bring more evils on those who are glorious on the earth.

Alleluia (3 times)

The Troparion

Tone 8
Women's Trio

Kievan Chant
D. Soloviev

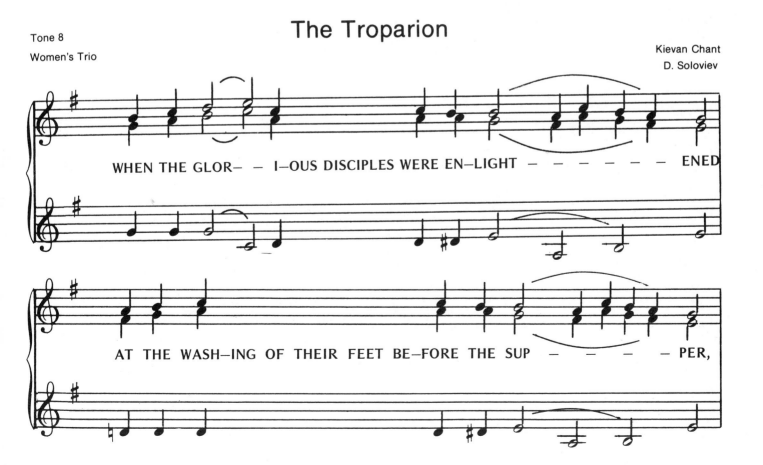

WHEN THE GLOR– — I–OUS DISCIPLES WERE EN–LIGHT — — — — — — ENED

AT THE WASH–ING OF THEIR FEET BE–FORE THE SUP — — — — PER,

Repeat: When the glorious disciples...

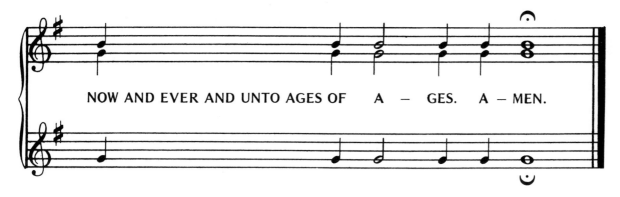

Repeat: When the glorious disciples...

Alleluia

Byzantine Chant

Tone 8

AL — — — LE — — — LU — I — — — A.

AL — — — LE — — — LU — — — I — — — A.

Verses:

In the night my soul rises early for Thee, O God, for Thy commandments are a light on the earth. *Alleluia (3 times)*

Learn righteousness, you inhabitants of the earth. *Alleluia (3 times)*

Jealousy shall grasp an untaught people. *Alleluia (3 times)*

Bring more evils on them, O Lord, bring more evils on those who are glorious on the earth. *Alleluia (3 times)*

The Troparion

Byzantine Chant

Tone 8

WHEN THE GLO — RI — OUS DIS — CI — PLES WERE EN — LIGHT — ENED AT

THE WASH—ING OF THEIR FEET BE—FORE THE SUP — — — — PER,

THEN THE IM — — PI — OUS JU — — DAS WAS DARK — — ENED,

AIL — ING WITH AV — — — A — RICE, AND TO THE LAW—LESS

JUDG — — ES HE BE–TRAYS THEE, THE RIGHT — EOUS

JUDGE. BE – HOLD O LOV — — ER OF MON — — EY, THIS MAN

WHO BE–CAUSE OF MON — EY HANGED HIM — — SELF.

FLEE FROM THE GREED–Y SOUL WHICH DARED SUCH THINGS

A–GAINST THE MAS — — — TER. O LORD, WHO ART GOOD

First ending:

TOWARDS ALL MEN, GLO — — RY TO THEE!

Final ending:

GLO — RY TO THEE!

Glory to the Father and to the Son and to the Holy Spirit. *When the glorious disciples....*
Now and ever and unto ages of ages. Amen. *When the glorious disciples....*

The Little Litany

Russian Chant

LORD, HAVE MER — CY.   TO THEE, O LORD   A — MEN.

The Little Litany

Znamenny Chant
A. Arkhangelsky

LORD, HAVE MER — CY.   TO THEE,   O   LORD.   A — MEN.

At the Gospel

At the Gospel

Priest: That we may be accounted worthy...

Russian Chant

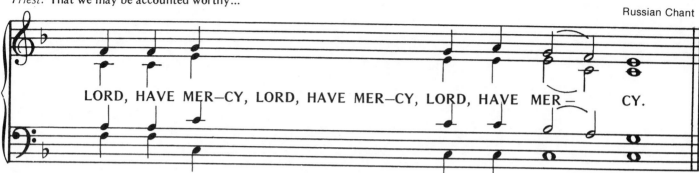

LORD, HAVE MER—CY, LORD, HAVE MER—CY, LORD, HAVE MER— CY.

Priest: Wisdom!...Peace be unto all!

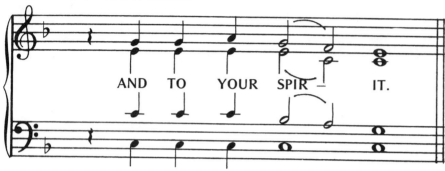

AND TO YOUR SPIR— IT.

Before the Gospel:

GLO—RY TO THY PAS—SION, O LORD.

After the Gospel:

GLO—RY TO THY LONG—SUF—FER—ING O LORD.

At the Gospel

Byzantine Chant

Antiphon I

Obikhod
N. Bakhmetev

Glory to the Father and to the Son and to the Holy Spirit, now and ever and unto ages of ages. Amen.

Tone 8

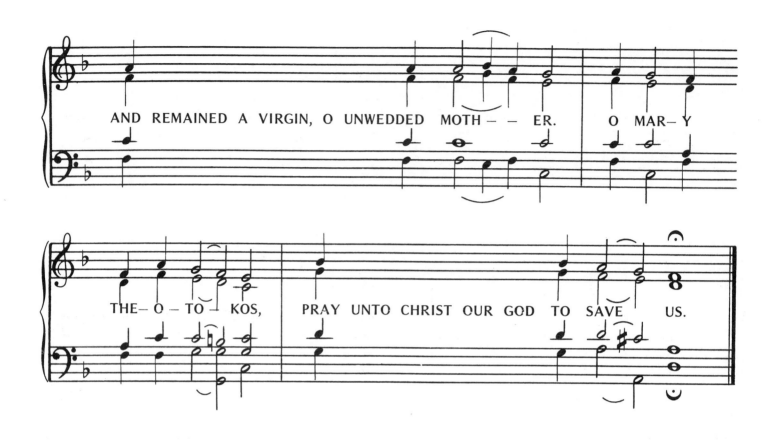

Antiphon II

Tone 6

Obikhod
N. Bakhmetev

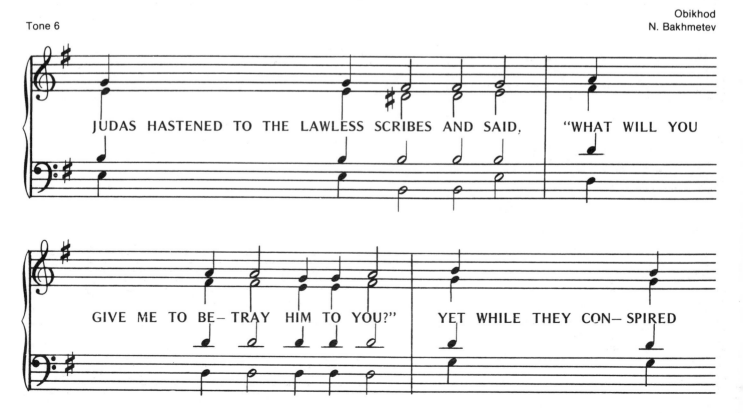

Glory to the Father and to the Son and to the Holy Spirit, now and ever and unto ages of ages. Amen.

Tone 6

NEVER CEASE TO PRAY TO HIM WHO LOVES MAN— KIND, WHO WAS

INEFFABLY BORN OF YOU, O VIR — GIN. THAT HE MAY SAVE FROM

DAN — GERS THOSE WHO TAKE RE— FUGE IN YOU.

Antiphon III

Obikhod
N. Bakhmetev

Tone 2

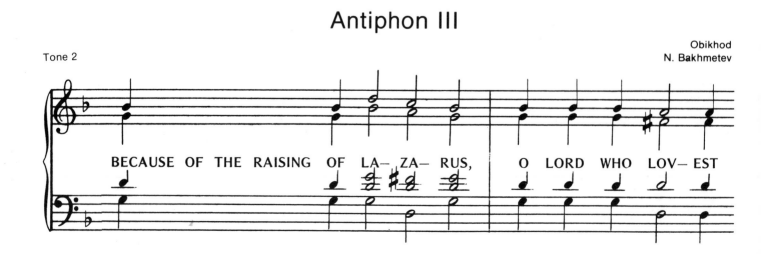

BECAUSE OF THE RAISING OF LA— ZA— RUS, O LORD WHO LOV— EST

MAN— KIND, THE HE— BREW CHILDREN CRIED "HO— SAN—NA" TO THEE,

Refrain:

BUT JUDAS THE TRANSGRESSOR WAS UN— WILL— ING TO UN— DER— STAND.

Tone 2

AT THY SUPPER, O CHRIST GOD, THOU DIDST ANNOUNCE TO THY

Refrain:

DIS— CI— PLES, "ONE OF YOU WILL BE— TRAY ME." BUT JUDAS

THE TRANSGRESSOR WAS UN— WILL— ING TO UN— DER— STAND.

Refrain:

TO THY DIS— CI— PLES, O OUR GOD, BUT JUDAS THE TRANSGRESSOR

WAS UN— WILL— ING TO UN— DER— STAND.

Glory to the Father and to the Son and to the Holy Spirit, now and ever and unto ages of ages. Amen.

Tone 2

O THE— O— TO— KOS, PRESERVE YOUR SERVANTS FROM DAN— GERS,

FOR AFTER GOD WE ALL TAKE RE— FUGE IN YOU AS AN INVINCIBLE

BULWARK AND PRO— TEC — — TOR.

The Little Litany

Russian Chant

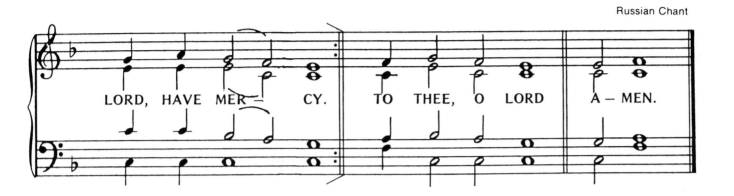

LORD, HAVE MER — CY. TO THEE, O LORD A — MEN.

The Little Litany

Znamenny Chant
A. Arkhangelsky

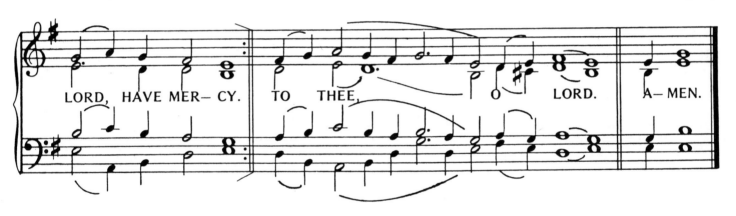

LORD, HAVE MER— CY. TO THEE, O LORD. A—MEN.

Kathisma Hymn

Tone 7

Obikhod
N. Bakhmetev

O LONG—SUFFERING LORD GLO—RY TO THEE.

Kathisma Hymn

Carpatho-Russian

Tone 7

WHEN THOU WAST FEED—ING THY DISCIPLES AT THE SUP — PER, THOU DIDST

KNOW JUD—AS' IN—TEN—TION TO BE —TRAY THEE; AND THOU DIDST

AC —CUSE HIM OF THIS, THOUGH RECOGNIZING HIM TO BE BE—YOND COR — REC — TION,

FOR THOU DIDST DESIRE ALL TO KNOW THAT THOU WAST WILL—ING—LY

BE—TRAYED TO SNATCH THE WORLD FROM THE GRASP OF THE EN — E — MY.

O LONG—SUF —FER—ING LORD, GLO — RY TO THEE!

At the Gospel

Priest: That we may be accounted worthy...

Kievan

LORD, HAVE MER—CY, LORD, HAVE MER—CY, LORD, HAVE MER — CY,

Priest: Wisdom!...Peace be unto all!

AND TO YOUR SPIR — — IT.

Before the Gospel:

GLO — RY TO THY PAS—SION O LORD, O LORD.

After the Gospel:

GLO — RY TO THY LONG-SUF—FER—ING O LORD,

O LORD.

Antiphon IV

Tone 5

Obikhod
N. Bakhmetev

TO—DAY JUDAS FORSAKES THE MAS—TER AND TAKES THE DE—VIL

AS HIS FRIEND. HE IS BLIND—ED BY THE PASSION OF AV—A—RICE.

DARK—ENED HE FALLS FROM THE LIGHT. HE SOLD THE SUN FOR

THIRTY PIECES OF SIL—VER. HOW, THEN, IS HE A—BLE TO SEE?

BUT HE WHO SUFFERS FOR THE WORLD HAS RISEN AS THE DAWN FOR US.

TO HIM LET US CRY A – LOUD: O THOU WHO SUFFEREST FOR US AND

WITH US, GLO – RY TO THEE !

Tone 5

TO–DAY JUDAS COUNTERFEITS PI–E–TY AND DEPRIVES HIMSELF OF THE GIFT

OF GRACE. THE DIS–CI–PLE BECOMES A BE–TRAY– ER. IN A GES–TURE

OF FRIENDSHIP HE CON–CEALS DE–CEIT. HE FOOLISHLY PREFERS THIRTY

PIECES OF SILVER TO THE MAS—TER'S LOVE AND BE—COMES A GUIDE FOR

THE LAW—LESS AS—SEM—BLY. BUT LET US GLORIFY CHRIST, OUR SAL—VA——TION.

Tone 1

AS BROTH—ERS IN CHRIST LET US AC—QUIRE BROTH—ER—LY LOVE.

LET US NOT LACK SYMPATHY FOR OUR NEIGH—BOR, LEST WE,

LIKE THE UN-MER-CI-FUL SER—VANT, BE CONDEMNED ON AC--COUNT OF

MON— EY, OR LIKE JUDAS GAIN NOTHING FROM OUR RE— GRETS.

Glory to the Father and to the Son and to the Holy Spirit, now and ever and unto ages of ages. Amen.

Tone 1

EV— ERY—WHERE GLORIOUS THINGS ARE SPO— KEN OF YOU, O MARY

THEOTOKOS, UN—WED—DED AND ALL—PRAISED, FOR YOU CONCEIVED

IN THE FLESH THE MAK— ER OF ALL.

Antiphon V

Tone 6

Obikhod
N. Bakhmetev

THE DISCIPLE AGREES UPON THE PRICE OF THE MAS—TER. HE SELLS THE LORD

FOR THIRTY PIECES OF SIL—VER. WITH A TREACHEROUS KISS HE BE—TRAYS

HIM TO DEATH AT THE HANDS OF LAW—LESS MEN.

Tone 6

TODAY THE CREATOR OF HEAV—EN AND EARTH SAID TO HIS DIS—CI—PLES,

"THE HOUR HAS COME AND JUDAS RUSHES TO BE—TRAY ME. LET NO ONE

DE—NY ME WHEN HE SEES ME ON THE CROSS BE—TWEEN TWO THIEVES.

FOR AS A MAN I SUF—FER, AND AS THE LOVER OF MAN I SAVE THOSE

WHO BE—LIEVE IN ME."

Glory to the Father and to the Son and to the Holy Spirit, now and ever and unto ages of ages. Amen.

Tone 6

O VIRGIN, WHO IN THE LAT—TER DAYS WONDROUSLY CONCEIVED AND BORE

YOUR OWN CRE—A—TOR, SAVE THOSE WHO MAG—NI—FY YOU.

Antiphon VI

Tone 7

Obikhod
N. Bakhmetev

Tone 7

TO— DAY HIS PEO—PLE NAIL TO THE CROSS   THE LORD WHO DIVIDED THE

SEA WITH A ROD AND LED THEM IN THE WIL— DER— NESS.   TO— DAY

THEY PIERCE HIS SIDE WITH A SPEAR   WHO SMOTE E— GYPT WITH PLAGUES

FOR THEIR SAKE.   THEY GIVE HIM GALL TO DRINK WHO RAINED DOWN

MAN— NA UP— ON THEM FOR FOOD.

Tone 7

WHEN THOU CA—MEST TO THY VOL—UN—TA—RY PAS—SION, O LORD,

THOU DIDST CRY TO THY DIS—CI—PLES: IF YOU LACK THE STRENGTH

TO KEEP WATCH WITH ME FOR A SIN—GLE HOUR, WHY DID YOU PROMISE TO

DIE FOR ME? SEE HOW JU—DAS DOES NOT SLEEP BUT HAS—TENS TO BETRAY

ME TO THE TRANS—GRES—SORS. A—RISE AND PRAY, LEST ANYONE DE—NY

49

ME WHEN HE SEES ME ON THE CROSS." O LONG–SUF–FER–ING ONE,

GLO– RY TO THEE!

Glory to the Father and to the Son and to the Holy Spirit,
now and ever and unto ages of ages. Amen.

Tone 7

RE–JOICE, O THE– O– TO– KOS, YOU HELD IN YOUR WOMB HIM WHOM THE

HEAV– ENS CAN– NOT HOLD. RE–JOICE, O VIR– GIN WHOM THE PRO–PHETS

PRO–CLAIMED, FROM YOU EMMANUEL HAS SHONE FORTH ON US.

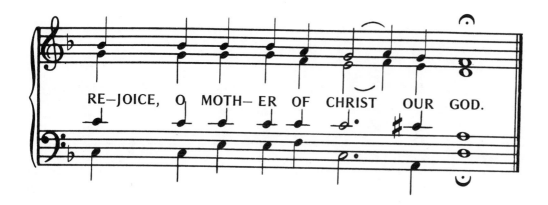

REJOICE, O MOTHER OF CHRIST OUR GOD.

The Little Litany

Russian Chant

LORD, HAVE MERCY. TO THEE, O LORD A-MEN.

The Little Litany

Znamenny Chant
A. Arkhangelsky

LORD, HAVE MER-CY. TO THEE, O LORD. A-MEN.

Kathisma Hymn

Obikhod
N. Bakhmetev

Tone 7

WHAT CAUSED YOU TO BETRAY THE SAVIOR, O JU— DAS? DID HE EX—PEL

YOU FROM THE RANKS OF THE A—POS—TLES? DID HE TAKE FROM

YOU THE GIFT OF HEAL—ING? DID HE SEND YOU FROM THE TABLE

WHILE TAKING SUPPER WITH THE OTH—ERS? DID HE WASH THEIR

FEET AND PASS YOU BY? HOW HAVE YOU FORGOTTEN SUCH GOOD THINGS?

YOUR IN—GRAT—I—TUDE IS NO—TOR—I—OUS, BUT HIS BOUNDLESS LONG—

SUFFERING AND GREAT MER—CY ARE PRO—CLAIMED TO ALL.

Kathisma Hymn

Tone 7

Carpatho-Russian

WHAT CAUSED YOU TO BETRAY THE SAV—IOR, O JUD — AS? DID HE

EX — PEL YOU FROM THE RANKS OF THE A — POS — TLES? DID HE

TAKE FROM YOU THE GIFT OF HEAL — ING? DID HE SEND YOU FROM

THE TABLE WHILE TAKING SUP—PER WITH THE OTH — ERS? DID HE WASH

THEIR FEET AND PASS YOU BY? HOW HAVE YOU FOR—GOT—TEN

SUCH GOOD THINGS? YOUR IN—GRAT—I—TUDE IS NO—TO — — — RI—OUS,

BUT HIS BOUND—LESS LONG—SUF—FER—ING AND GREAT MER — CY ARE

PRO—CLAIMED TO ALL.

At the Gospel

Antiphon VII

Tone 8

Obikhod
N. Bakhmetev

WHILE PER—MIT—TING TRANSGRESSORS TO AR—REST THEE, THOU DIDST CRY OUT

TO THEM, O LORD: "THOUGH YOU SMITE THE SHEPHERD AND SCATTER THE

TWELVE SHEEP, MY DIS—CI—PLES, I AM ABLE TO SURROUND MYSELF WITH

MORE THAN THIRTY LEGIONS OF AN—GELS. BUT I FORE—BEAR

SO THAT THE SECRET AND HIDDEN THINGS MIGHT BE FUL—FILLED

56

WHICH WERE REVEALED TO YOU BY MY PRO—PHETS." O LORD,

GLO—RY TO THEE!

Tone 8

DE—NY—ING THEE FOR THE THIRD TIME, PETER AT ONCE RECALLED

THY WORDS TO HIM, BUT HE OFFERED THEE TEARS OF RE—PEN—TANCE:

O GOD, HAVE MERCY ON ME AND SAVE ME!

Glory to the Father and to the Son and to the Holy Spirit, now and ever and unto ages of ages. Amen.

Tone 8

LET US PRAISE THE HO—LY VIR—GIN, AS THE GATE OF SALVATION AND

FAIR PAR—A—DISE, AS A CLOUD FOR THE E—TER—NAL LIGHT.

TO HER LET US ALL SAY, "RE—JOICE!"

Antiphon VIII

Obikhod
N. Bakhmetev

Tone 2

O TRANS—GRES—SORS, WHAT HAVE YOU HEARD FROM OUR SA—VIOR?

DID HE NOT EX-PLAIN THE LAW AND THE TEACHINGS OF THE PRO-PHETS?

WHY THEN DID YOU PLAN TO DELIVER TO PI-LATE THE WORD, GOD OF GOD,

THE RE-DEEM-ER OF OUR SOULS?

Tone 2

"LET HIM BE CRU-CI-FIED," CRIED THOSE WHO HAD ALWAYS ENJOYED

HIS GRA-CIOUS GIFTS. THOSE WHO KILLED THE RIGHT-EOUS ASK TO

RECEIVE A MAL—E—FAC—TOR INSTEAD OF THEIR BE— NE— FAC— TOR. BUT THOU,

O CHRIST, DIDST ENDURE THEIR HEEDLESSNESS IN SI—LENCE, DESIRING TO

SUFFER AND TO SAVE US IN THY LOVE FOR MAN— KIND.

Glory to the Father and to the Son and to the Holy Spirit, now and ever and unto ages of ages. Amen.

Tone 2

WE HAVE NO BOLD — NESS BECAUSE OF THE MUL—TI—TUDE OF OUR SINS,

BUT EN— TREAT HIM WHO WAS BORN OF YOU, O VIRGIN THE— O — TO—KOS,

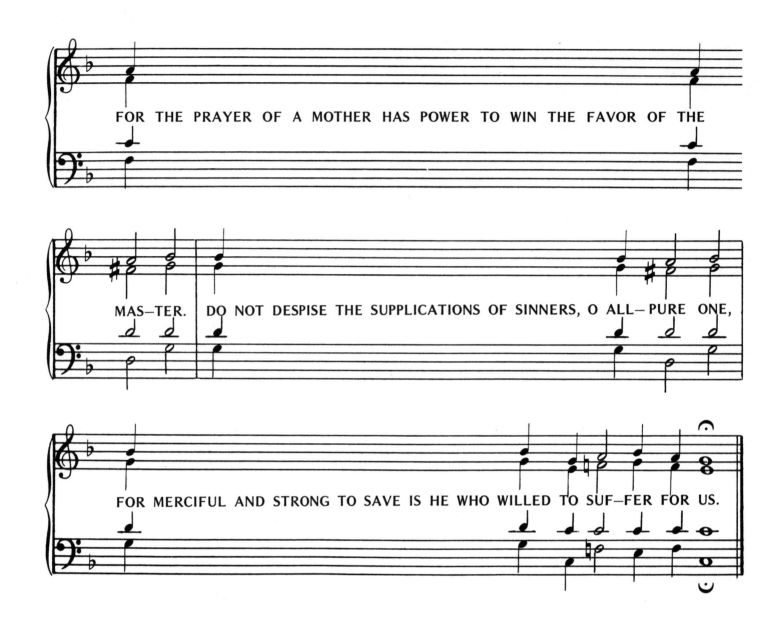

FOR THE PRAYER OF A MOTHER HAS POWER TO WIN THE FAVOR OF THE MAS-TER. DO NOT DESPISE THE SUPPLICATIONS OF SINNERS, O ALL—PURE ONE, FOR MERCIFUL AND STRONG TO SAVE IS HE WHO WILLED TO SUF—FER FOR US.

Antiphon IX

Obikhod
N. Bakhmetev

Tone 3

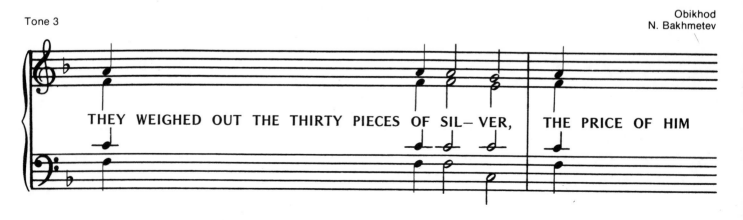

THEY WEIGHED OUT THE THIRTY PIECES OF SIL—VER, THE PRICE OF HIM

62

TO DRINK. BUT DO THOU, O LORD, RAISE ME UP THAT I MAY RE-QUITE THEM.

Glory to the Father and to the Son and to the Holy Spirit, now and ever and unto ages of ages. Amen.

Tone 3

WE THE GENTILES PRAISE YOU, O PURE THE-O-TO-KOS, FOR YOU GAVE

BIRTH TO CHRIST OUR GOD, WHO THROUGH YOU FREED MAN-KIND

FROM THE CURSE.

The Little Litany

Russian Chant

LORD, HAVE MER — CY.   TO THEE, O LORD   A — MEN.

The Little Litany

Znamenny Chant
A. Arkhangelsky

LORD, HAVE MER — CY.   TO THEE,   O   LORD.   A — MEN.

Kathisma Hymn

Tone 8

Obikhod
N. Bakhmetev

HOW COULD JU—DAS, WHO WAS ONCE THY DIS—CI — PLE, PLAN TO BE— TRAY

THEE. THAT TREACHEROUS AND UNRIGHTEOUS MAN DE—CEIT—FUL—LY ATE

WITH THEE AND WENT TO THE PRIESTS AND SAID: "WHAT WILL YOU GIVE

ME IF I DE—LIV—ER TO YOU HIM WHO ABOLISHED THE LAW AND PRO—FANED

THE SAB— BATH?" O LONG—SUFFERING LORD, GLO—RY TO THEE!

Kathisma Hymn

Tone 8

Carpatho-Russian

HOW COULD JUD—AS, WHO WAS ONCE THY DIS — CI — — — — — PLE,

PLAN TO BE—TRAY THEE? THAT TREACH-ER — OUS AND

UN—RIGHT—EOUS MAN DE—CEIT—FUL—LY ATE WITH THEE

AND WENT TO THE PRIESTS AND SAID: "WHAT WILL YOU GIVE

ME IF I DE—LIV — — ER TO YOU HIM WHO A—BOL—ISHED

THE LAW AND PRO-FANED THE SAB — — —BATH?" O LONG—

—SUF — FER—ING LORD, GLO — RY TO THEE!

At the Gospel

Antiphon X

Obikhod
N. Bakhmetev

Tone 6

HE WHO CLOTHES HIMSELF WITH LIGHT AS WITH A GAR—MENT STOOD NA—KED

FOR TRIAL. HE WAS STRUCK ON THE CHEEK BY HANDS THAT HE HIM—SELF

HAD FORMED. A PEOPLE THAT TRANS—GRESSED THE LAW NAILED THE LORD

OF GLO—RY TO THE CROSS. THEN THE CURTAIN OF THE TEMPLE WAS TORN

IN TWO. THEN THE SUN WAS DARK—ENED, UNABLE TO BEAR THE SIGHT OF GOD

OUT—RAGED, BEFORE WHOM ALL THINGS TREM—BLE. LET US WOR—SHIP HIM.

Tone 6

THE DISCIPLE DE—NIED HIM, BUT THE THIEF CRIED OUT: "REMEMBER ME,

O LORD, IN THY KING—DOM!"

Glory to the Father and to the Son and to the Holy Spirit, now and ever and unto ages of ages. Amen.

Tone 6

O LORD, WHO FOR THY SER—VANTS' SAKE DIDST WILL TO TAKE FLESH FROM THE

VIR—GIN, GRANT PEACE TO THE WORLD, THAT WITH ONE VOICE WE MAY

Antiphon XI

Tone 6

Obikhod
N. Bakhmetev

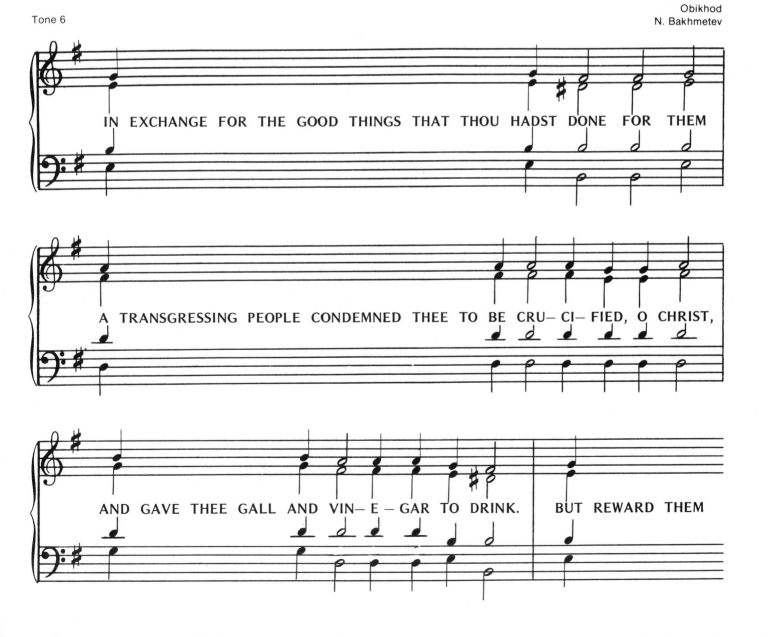

Tone 6

PLOTTED A—GAINST THEE IN VAIN.

Tone 6

NEITHER THE SHAKING OF THE EARTH NOR THE SPLIT—TING OF THE ROCKS,

NEITHER THE TEARING OF THE TEMPLE'S CURTAIN NOR THE RE—SUR—REC—TION

OF THE DEAD CONVINCED A TRANSGRESSING PEO— PLE. BUT REWARD

THEM ACCORDING TO THEIR DEEDS, O LORD, FOR THEY PLOTTED A—GAINST

THEE IN VAIN.

Glory to the Father and to the Son and to the Holy Spirit,
now and ever and unto ages of ages. Amen.

Tone 6

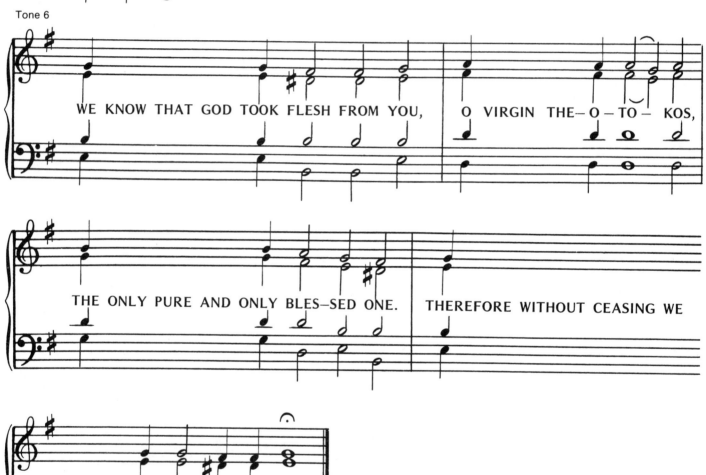

WE KNOW THAT GOD TOOK FLESH FROM YOU, O VIRGIN THE–O–TO–KOS,

THE ONLY PURE AND ONLY BLES–SED ONE. THEREFORE WITHOUT CEASING WE

PRAISE AND MAG–NI–FY YOU.

Antiphon XII

Obikhod
N. Bakhmetev

Tone 8

THUS SAYS THE LORD TO THE JEWS: "MY PEOPLE, WHAT HAVE I DONE TO YOU,

OR HOW HAVE I OF—FEND—ED YOU? TO YOUR BLIND I GAVE SIGHT, YOUR

LEP—ERS I CLEANSED, THE PARALYTIC I RAISED FROM HIS BED. MY PEOPLE,

WHAT HAVE I DONE TO YOU, AND HOW HAVE YOU RE—PAID ME? INSTEAD

OF MANNA, GALL; INSTEAD OF WATER, VIN—E—GAR; INSTEAD OF LOVING ME,

74

Tone 8

SEEING THE MAS—TER CRU—CI—FIED.

Tone 8

THE CHOIR OF THE APOSTLES CRIES OUT TO YOU, O LAWGIVERS OF ISRAEL,

SCRIBES AND PHAR—I—SEES: BE—HOLD THE TEM—PLE WHICH YOU DES—TROYED!

BEHOLD THE LAMB WHOM YOU CRU—CI—FIED! YOU DELIVERED HIM TO THE

TOMB, BUT BY HIS OWN POW—ER HE A—ROSE. DO NOT BE DE—CEIVED, O JEWS.

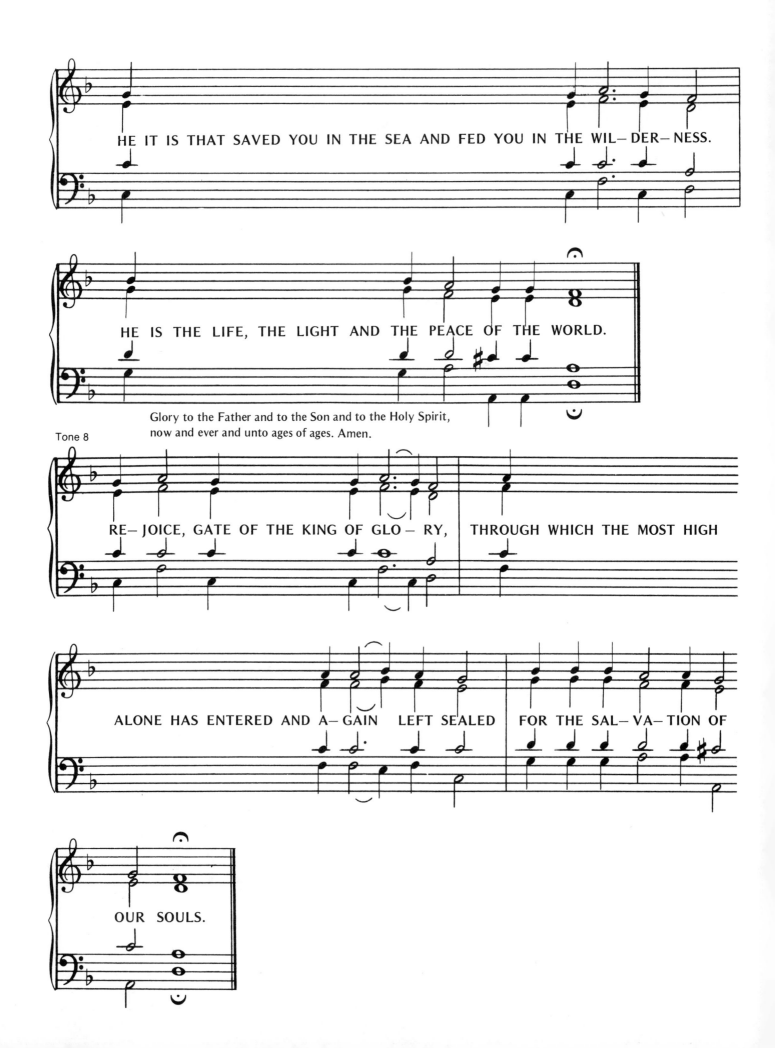

HE IT IS THAT SAVED YOU IN THE SEA AND FED YOU IN THE WIL—DER—NESS.

HE IS THE LIFE, THE LIGHT AND THE PEACE OF THE WORLD.

Glory to the Father and to the Son and to the Holy Spirit,
now and ever and unto ages of ages. Amen.

Tone 8

RE—JOICE, GATE OF THE KING OF GLO—RY, THROUGH WHICH THE MOST HIGH

ALONE HAS ENTERED AND A—GAIN LEFT SEALED   FOR THE SAL—VA—TION OF

OUR SOULS.

The Little Litany

Russian Chant

The Little Litany

Znamenny Chant
A. Arkhangelsky

Kathisma Hymn

Tone 8

Obikhod
N. Bakhmetev

Kathisma Hymn

Tone 8

Carpatho-Russian

O GOD, THOU DIDST STAND BEFORE CA — IA — — — — PHAS.

O JUDGE, THOU WAST GIVEN O—VER TO PI — — — LATE. THEN THE

HEAV—EN—LY POW—ERS SHOOK WITH FEAR. THOUGH SIN — LESS,

THOU WAST NUMBERED AMONG THE TRANS-GRES — — — SORS, LIFT—ED

UP ON THE WOOD BE—TWEEN TWO THIEVES IN OR — DER TO

SAVE MAN — KIND. O PA — TIENT LORD, GLO — RY TO THEE!

At the Gospel

Antiphon XIII

Obikhod
N. Bakhmetev

Tone 6

THE CROWD OF THE JEWS, O LORD, ASKED PILATE TO CRU—CI—FY THEE,

AND THOUGH THEY FOUND NO GUILT IN THEE, THEY FREED BARABBAS, WHO

IN—DEED WAS GUIL—TY. THEY CONDEMNED THEE, THE RIGHT—EOUS ONE,

AND MADE THE CHARGE OF MURDER THEIR IN—HER—I—TANCE. BUT GIVE THEM

THEIR RE—TRI—BU—TION, O LORD, FOR THEY PLOTTED A—GAINST THEE IN VAIN.

82

OWN CRE—A——TOR, ENTREAT HIM TO SAVE OUR SOULS.

Antiphon XIV

Tone 8

Obikhod
N. Bakhmetev

THE THIEF, WHOSE HANDS WERE DE—FILED WITH BLOOD, THOU DIDST ACCEPT

AS THY FELLOW—TRAV —EL—ER. WITH HIM NUM—BER US AL—SO, O LORD,

FOR THOU ART GOOD AND LOV—EST MAN—KIND.

84

Glory to the Father and to the Son and to the Holy Spirit, now and ever and unto ages of ages. Amen.

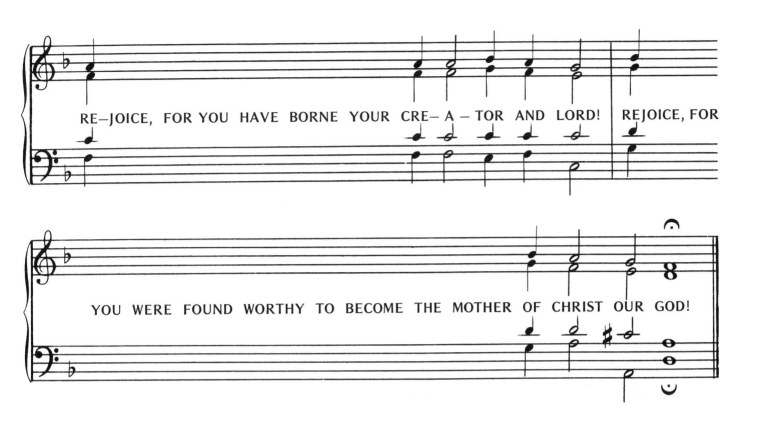

RE–JOICE, FOR YOU HAVE BORNE YOUR CRE– A – TOR AND LORD! REJOICE, FOR

YOU WERE FOUND WORTHY TO BECOME THE MOTHER OF CHRIST OUR GOD!

Antiphon XV

Obikhod
N. Bakhmetev

Tone 6

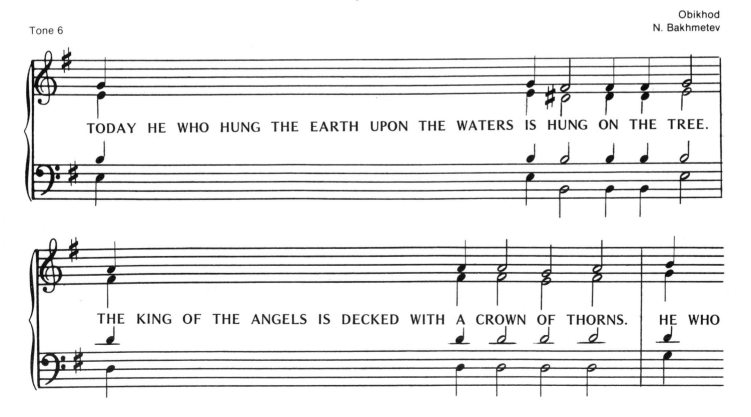

TODAY HE WHO HUNG THE EARTH UPON THE WATERS IS HUNG ON THE TREE.

THE KING OF THE ANGELS IS DECKED WITH A CROWN OF THORNS. HE WHO

86

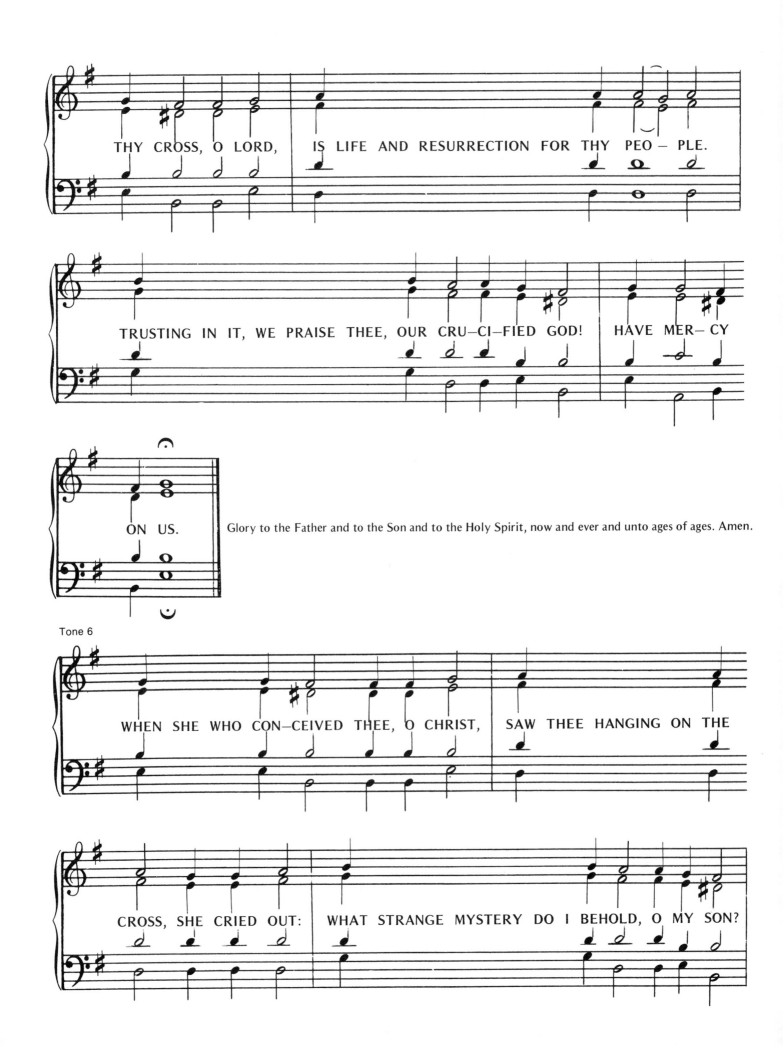

THY CROSS, O LORD, IS LIFE AND RESURRECTION FOR THY PEO—PLE.

TRUSTING IN IT, WE PRAISE THEE, OUR CRU—CI—FIED GOD! HAVE MER—CY

ON US. Glory to the Father and to the Son and to the Holy Spirit, now and ever and unto ages of ages. Amen.

Tone 6

WHEN SHE WHO CON—CEIVED THEE, O CHRIST, SAW THEE HANGING ON THE

CROSS, SHE CRIED OUT: WHAT STRANGE MYSTERY DO I BEHOLD, O MY SON?

O GIVER OF LIFE, HOW DOST THOU DIE, NAILED ON THE WOOD IN THE FLESH?

Antiphon XV

TO—DAY HE WHO HUNG THE EARTH UP—ON

THE WA — — — TERS IS HUNG UP—ON

THE TREE. TO—DAY HE WHO HUNG THE

EARTH UP—ON THE WA — — — — — TERS IS HUNG

UP – ON THE TREE. TO – DAY HE WHO

HUNG THE EARTH UP – ON THE WA – – – – TERS IS

HUNG UP – ON THE TREE. THE KING OF THE

AN – GELS IS DECKED WITH A CROWN OF THORNS.

HE WHO WRAPS THE HEAV'NS WITH CLOUDS IS WRAPPED IN

THE PUR – PLE OF MOCK – – ER – Y. HE WHO FREED

AD – AM IN THE JOR – DAN IS SLAPPED ON THE FACE.

The Little Litany

Russian Chant

LORD, HAVE MER — CY.   TO THEE, O LORD   A — MEN.

The Little Litany

Znamenny Chant
A. Arkhangelsky

LORD, HAVE MER— CY.   TO THEE,   O   LORD.   A—MEN.

Kathisma Hymn

Obikhod
N. Bakhmetev

BY THY PRE—CIOUS BLOOD THOU HAST REDEEMED US FROM THE CURSE

OF THE LAW. BY BE—ING NAILED TO THE CROSS AND PIERCED BY A SPEAR

THOU HAST POURED FORTH IM—MOR—TAL—I—TY FOR MAN. O OUR SAV—IOR,

GLO—RY TO THEE!

Kathisma Hymn

Tone 4

After Kastalsky

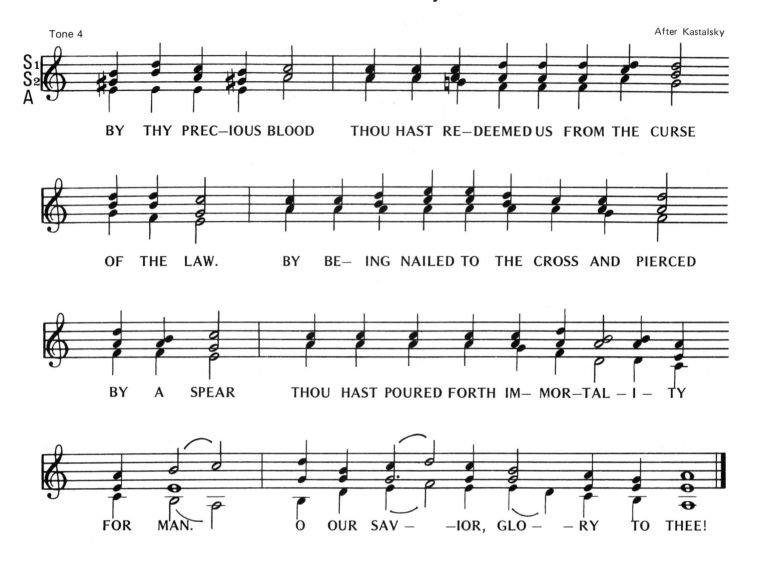

BY THY PREC—IOUS BLOOD THOU HAST RE—DEEMED US FROM THE CURSE

OF THE LAW. BY BE— ING NAILED TO THE CROSS AND PIERCED

BY A SPEAR THOU HAST POURED FORTH IM— MOR—TAL —I— TY

FOR MAN. O OUR SAV — —IOR, GLO — —RY TO THEE!

For additional settings, cf. pages 176 and 177.

At the Gospel

The Beatitudes — Verses

Choir: In Thy kingdom remember us, O Lord, when Thou comest in Thy kingdom.
Blessed are the poor in spirit, for theirs is the kingdom of heaven.
Blessed are those who mourn, for they shall be comforted.
Blessed are the meek, for they shall inherit the earth.

Reader:

Through a tree Adam lost his home in paradise, but through the tree of the cross the thief came there to dwell. By tasting of the truit, the first broke the Creator's commandment, but He who was crucified with Thee confessed Thee, the hidden God. Remember us also, O Savior, in Thy kingdom!

Choir: Blessed are those who hunger and thirst after righteousness, for they shall be filled.

Reader:

Lawless men bought the Creator of the law from a disciple and brought Him before the judgment seat of Pilate as a transgressor. Thou He had given them manna in the wilderness, they cried out: Crucify Him! But we, imitating the righteous thief, cry out in faith: Remember us also, O Savior, in Thy kingdom!

Choir: Blessed are the merciful, for they shall obtain mercy.

Reader:

The swarm of those who would kill God, the lawless nation of the Jews, cried out in fury to Pilate: Crucify Him! — Christ, the innocent one. And they sought instead the release of Barabbas. But with the wise thief we lift up our voices: Remember us also, O Savior, in Thy kingdom!

Choir: Blessed are the pure in heart, for they shall see God.

Reader:

From Thy life-bearing side, O Christ, a fountain flows forth as from Eden, giving drink to Thy Church as to a living paradise. From there it divided to become the four rivers of the Gospels, watering the world, gladdening creation, and teaching the nations to worship Thy kingdom in faith.

Choir: Blessed are the peacemakers, for they shall be called the sons of God.

Reader:

Thou wast crucified for my sake, in order to pour forth forgiveness for me. Thy side was pierced so that streams of life might flow for me. Thy hands were transfixed by nails so that, convinced of the height of Thy power by the depth of Thy sufferings, I might cry out to Thee, O Christ, Thou giver of life: Glory to Thy cross and to Thy Passion, O Savior!

Choir: Blessed are those who are persecuted for righteousness' sake for theirs is the kingdom of heaven.

Reader:

When it beheld Thee crucified, O Christ, all creation trembled. The foundations of the earth shook for fear of Thy might. The lights of heaven hid themselves, and the curtain of the temple was torn in two. The mountains quaked, and the rocks were split, and with us the believing thief cried out to Thee, O Savior: Remember me in Thy kingdom!

Choir: Blessed are you when men shall revile you and persecute you, and shall say all manner of evil against you falsely for my sake.

Reader:

On the cross Thou didst destroy the legal bond against us, O Lord. Thou wast reckoned with the dead and there didst bind the tyrant, delivering all from the bonds of death by Thy resurrection. By it we have been illumined, O Lord who lovest mankind, and we cry out to Thee: Remember us also, O Savior, in Thy kingdom!

Choir: Rejoice and be exceedingly glad, for great is your reward in heaven.

Reader:

Thou wast lifted up upon the cross, O Lord. Thou didst destroy the power of death, and as God Thou didst cancel the legal bond against us. Grant the repentance of the thief also unto us who worship Thee in faith, O only lover of mankind, and who cry out to Thee, O Christ our God: Remember us also, O Savior, in Thy kingdom!

Choir: Glory to the Father, and to the Son, and to the Holy Spirit.

Reader:

Let us, the faithful, all pray that with one voice we may worthily glorify the Father, the Son, and the Holy Spirit: One God existing in three persons yet remaining unconfused, simple, undivided, and unapproachable; by Whom we escape the flames of punishment.

Choir: Now and ever, and unto ages of ages. Amen.

Reader:

We offer to Thee as an intercessor, O Christ, Thy mother who bore Thee in the flesh without seed, the true virgin who after giving birth remained incorrupt. Through her intercessions, O most merciful Master, grant forgiveness of sins to us who cry unceasingly: Remember us also, O Savior, in Thy kingdom!

The Beatitudes

✱ *Insert Verses from pp. 96-97*

Carpatho-Russian

Matt. 5:3-12

IN THY KING—DOM RE—MEM—BER US, O LORD, WHEN THOU COM—EST IN THY KING — DOM. BLESS—ED ARE THE POOR IN SPIR — — IT, FOR THEIRS IS THE KING — DOM OF HEAV — EN. BLESS—ED ARE THOSE WHO MOURN, FOR THEY SHALL BE COM—FORT—ED. BLESS—ED ARE THE MEEK, FOR THEY SHALL IN—HER — IT THE EARTH. BLESS—ED

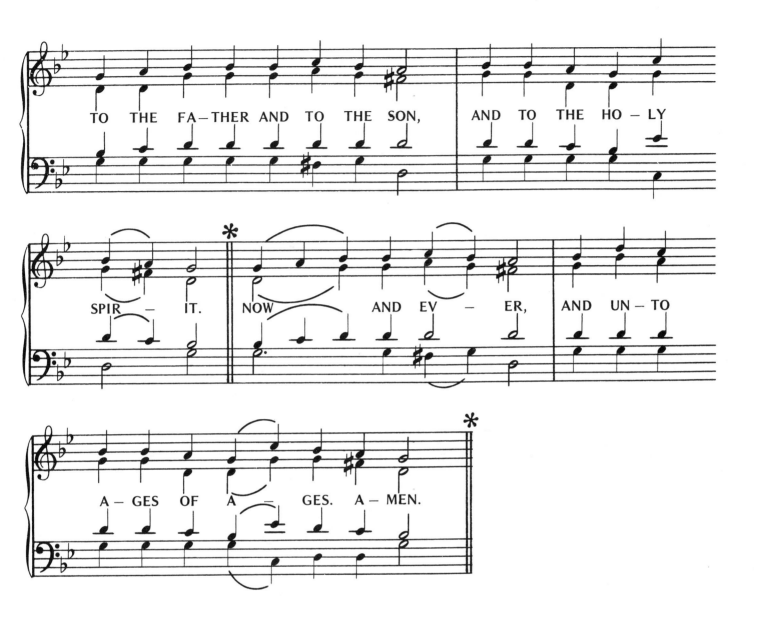

102

The Beatitudes

✱ *Insert Verses from pp. 96-97*

Matt. 5:3-12

Russian Chant

IN THY KING—DOM RE—MEM—BER US, O LORD, WHEN THOU

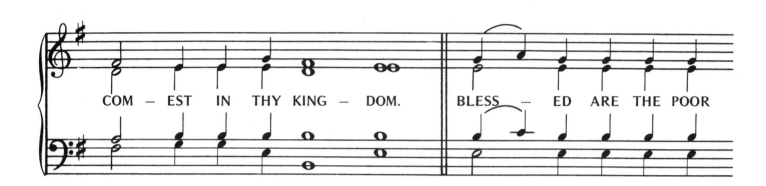

COM—EST IN THY KING—DOM. BLESS—ED ARE THE POOR

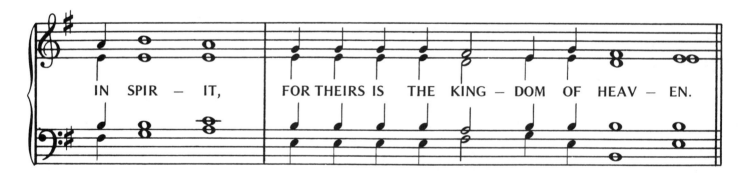

IN SPIR—IT, FOR THEIRS IS THE KING—DOM OF HEAV—EN.

BLESS—ED ARE THOSE WHO MOURN, FOR THEY SHALL BE

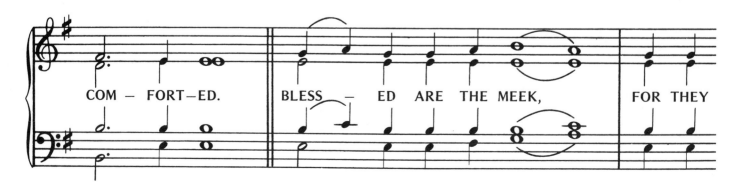

COM—FORT—ED. BLESS—ED ARE THE MEEK, FOR THEY

105

The Little Litany

Russian Chant

LORD, HAVE MER— CY. TO THEE, O LORD A — MEN.

The Little Litany

Znamenny Chant
A. Arkhangelsky

LORD, HAVE MER— CY. TO THEE, O LORD. A—MEN.

The Prokeimenon

Obikhod
N. Bakhmetev

Tone 4

Psalm 22:18

THEY DIVIDE MY GARMENTS AMONG THEM, AND FOR MY RAI — — — —

—MENT THEY CAST LOTS.

Verse: MY GOD, MY GOD, LOOK UPON ME! WHY HAST THOU FORSAKEN ME?

The Prokeimenon

Znamenny Chant
A. Arkhangelsky

Tone 4

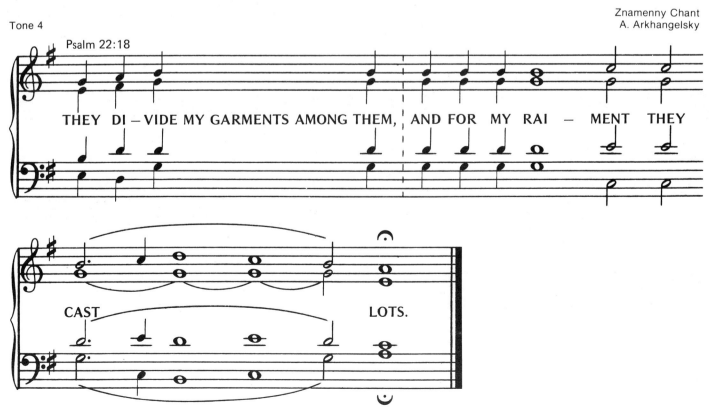

Psalm 22:18

THEY DI — VIDE MY GARMENTS AMONG THEM, AND FOR MY RAI — MENT THEY

CAST LOTS.

Verse: MY GOD, MY GOD, LOOK UPON ME! WHY HAST THOU FORSAKEN ME?

At the Gospel

Psalm 51

Have mercy on me, O God, according to Thy great mercy; according to the multitude of Thy tender mercies, blot out my transgressions. Wash me thoroughly from my iniquity, and cleanse me from my sin!

For I know my transgressions, and my sin is ever before me. Against Thee, Thee only, have I sinned, and done that which is evil in Thy sight, so that Thou art justified in Thy sentence and blameless in Thy judgment. Behold I was brought forth in iniquity, and in sin did my mother conceive me.

Behold, Thou desirest truth in the inward being; therefore teach me wisdom in my secret heart. Purge me with hyssop, and I shall be clean; wash me, and I shall be whiter than snow. Fill me with joy and gladness; let the bones which Thou hast broken rejoice. Hide Thy face from my sins, and blot out all my iniquities.

Create in me a clean heart, O God, and put a new and right spirit within me. Cast me not away from Thy presence, and take not Thy holy spirit from me. Restore to me the joy of Thy salvation, and uphold me with a willing spirit.

Then I will teach transgressors Thy ways, and sinners will return to Thee. Deliver me from blood-guiltiness, O God, Thou God of my salvation, and my tongue will sing aloud of Thy deliverance.

O Lord, open Thou my lips, and my mouth shall show forth Thy praise. For Thou hast no delight in sacrifice; were I to give a burnt offering, Thou wouldst not be pleased. The sacrifice acceptable to God is a broken spirit; a broken and contrite heart, O God, Thou wilt not despise.

Do good to Zion in Thy good pleasure; rebuild the walls of Jerusalem, then wilt Thou delight in right sacrifices, in burnt offerings and whole burnt offerings; then bulls will be offered on Thy altar.

At the Gospel

The Kanon — Ode 5

Heirmos
Tone 6

Znamenny Chant
Klimov-Lebedev

The Kanon — Ode 5

Heirmos
Tone 6

Znamenny Chant
P. Turchaninov

EAR - LY WILL I SEEK THEE O WORD OF GOD WHO WITH - OUT CHANGE DIDST EMP — — — TY THY - -SELF IN THY COM - -PAS - SION FOR FALL - - - EN MAN WHO WITH - OUT SUF -FER-

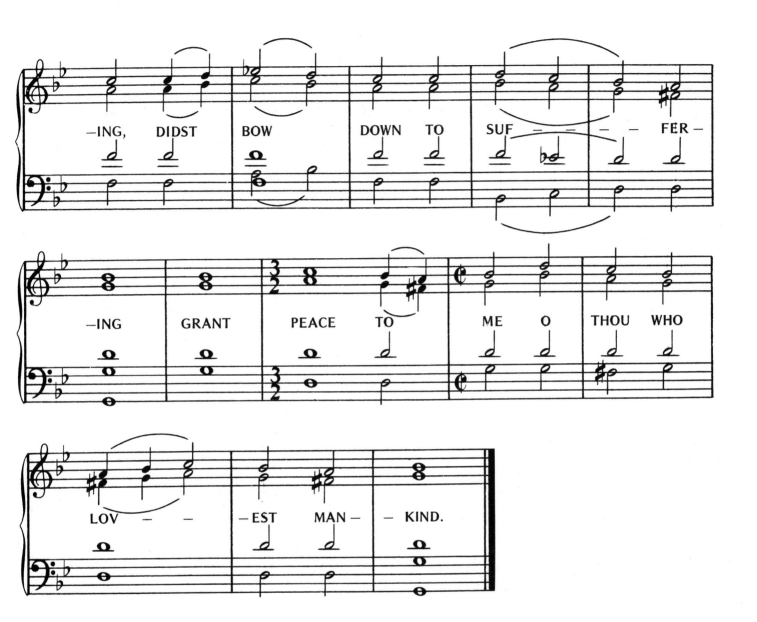

The Little Litany

Russian Chant

LORD, HAVE MER — CY. TO THEE, O LORD A — MEN.

The Little Litany

Znamenny Chant
A. Arkhangelsky

LORD, HAVE MER— CY. TO THEE, O LORD. A—MEN.

The Kontakion

Obikhod
N. Bakhmetev

Tone 8

COME LET US ALL SING THE PRAIS—ES OF HIM WHO WAS CRU — CI — FIED FOR US, FOR MA — RY SAID WHEN SHE BEHELD HIM UP — ON THE TREE: THOUGH THOU DOST EN — DURE THE CROSS, THOU ART MY SON AND MY GOD.

OIKOS ENDING:

THOU ART MY SON AND MY GOD.

The Kontakion

Tone 8

A. Kastalsky

COME LET US ALL SING THE PRAIS—ES OF HIM WHO WAS CRU — CI — FIED

FOR US, FOR MA — RY SAID WHEN SHE BE—HELD HIM UP — ON

THE TREE: THOUGH THOU DOST EN — DURE THE CROSS, THOU ART MY SON

AND MY GOD.

OIKOS ENDING:

THOU ART MY SON AND MY GOD.

The Kanon — Ode 8

Heirmos
Tone 6

Znamenny Chant
Klimov-Lebedev

THE GOD—LY YOUTHS EXPOSED A MONUMENT OF GOD—LESS WICK — ED—NESS,

BUT THE LAWLESS ASSEMBLY IS ENRAGED AND TAKES VAIN COUN-SEL A—GAINST

CHRIST. THEY PLAN TO KILL HIM WHO HOLDS LIFE IN THE PALM

OF HIS HAND, WHOM ALL CREATION BLESSES AND GLO — RI — FIES THROUGH-

-OUT ALL A — — GES.

The Kanon — Ode 8

Heirmos
Tone 6

Znamenny Chant
P. Turchaninov

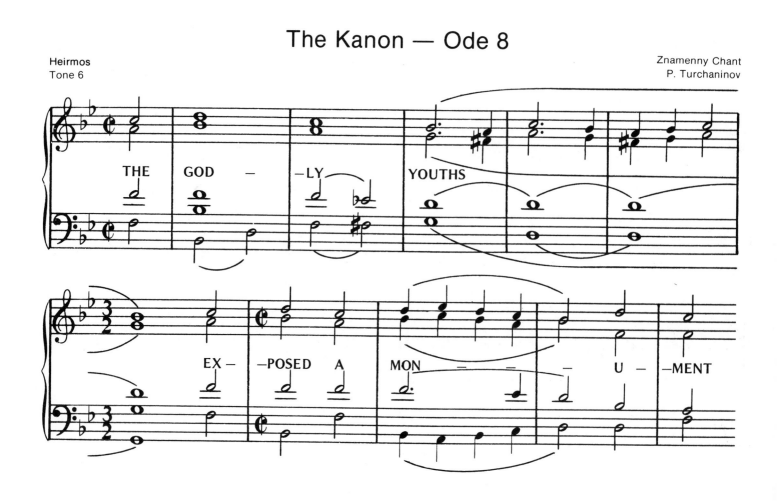

ALL CRE — —A — TION BLESS — —ES AND GLO —

— —RI — —FIES THROUGH— —OUT ALL A —

—GES.

After Turchaninov

WE PRAISE, BLESS, AND WORSHIP THE LORD, SINGING AND EXALTING HIM

THROUGH— —OUT ALL A — — —GES.

The Kanon — Ode 9

Heirmos
Tone 6

Znamenny Chant
Klimov-Lebedev

MORE HON'—RA—BLE THAN THE CHE—RU—BIM, AND MORE GLO—RI—OUS

BE—YOND COMPARE THAN THE SER — — A — PHIM, WITH—OUT DE —

—FILE — MENT YOU GAVE BIRTH TO GOD THE WORD; TRUE THE—

—O — TO—KOS, WE MAG — —NI—FY YOU.

The Kanon — Ode 9

Heirmos
Tone 6

Znamenny Chant
P. Turchaninov

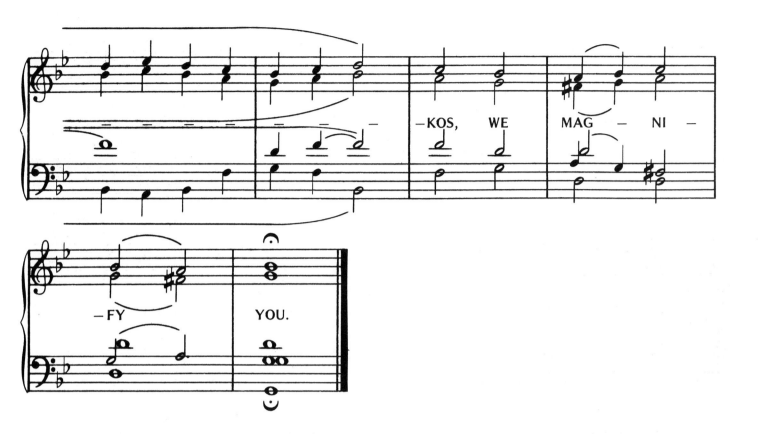

124

The Exapostilarion — The Wise Thief

Kievo-Pecherskaya Lavra

THE WISE THIEF DIDST THOU MAKE WOR — — THY OF PAR — — —

—A — DISE IN A SIN—GLE MO — — MENT, O LORD. BY THE WOOD

OF THY CROSS, IL — LU — MINE ME AS WELL, AND SAVE ME!

The Exapostilarion — The Wise Thief

H. Benigsen/J. Erickson

THE WISE THIEF DIDST THOU MAKE WOR — THY OF PAR — A — DISE IN A SIN—GLE MO — MENT, O LORD: BY THE WOOD OF THY CROSS, IL- —LU-MINE ME AS WELL, AND SAVE ME.

The Exapostilarion — The Wise Thief

Staritsky

THE WISE THIEF DIDST THOU MAKE WOR- -THY OF PAR - - A - DISE IN A SIN - GLE MO - MENT, A SIN - GLE MO - MENT, O LORD: BY THE WOOD OF THY CROSS, IL - LU - MINE ME AS WELL, AND SAVE ME, AND SAVE ME!

The Exapostilarion — The Wise Thief

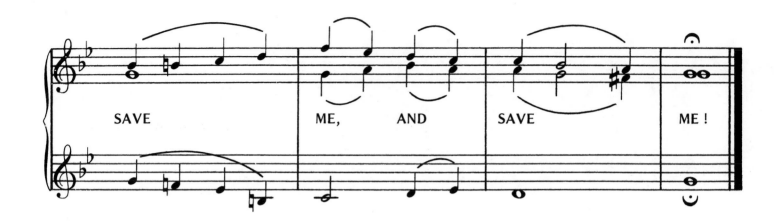

SAVE   ME,   AND   SAVE   ME !

The Exapostilarion — The Wise Thief

Byzantine Chant

THE WISE THIEF DIDST THOU MAKE WOR — — — THY OF PAR — A — DISE

IN A SIN — — GLE MO — MENT, O LORD. BY THE WOOD

OF THY CROSS, IL — LU — MINE ME AS WELL, AND SAVE ME !

The Exapostilarion — The Wise Thief

Kievan Chant
B. Ledkovsky

The Exapostilarion — The Wise Thief

B. Ledkovsky

At the Gospel

Kievan

The Praises

Psalms 148, 149, and 150

READER: Praise the Lord from the heavens, praise Him in the heights! Praise Him, all His angels; praise Him, all His host!

Praise Him, sun and moon; praise Him, all you shining stars! Praise Him, you highest heavens, and you waters above the heavens!

Let them praise the name of the Lord! For He commanded and they were created. And He established them for ever and ever; He fixed their bounds which cannot be passed.

Praise the Lord from the earth, you sea monsters and all deeps, fire and hail, snow and frost, stormy wind fulfilling His command!

Mountains and all hills, fruit trees and all cedars! Beasts and all cattle, creeping things and flying birds!

Kings of the earth and all peoples, princes and all rulers of the earth! Young men and maidens together, old men and children!

Let them praise the name of the Lord, for His name alone is exalted; His glory is above earth and heaven.

He has raised up a horn for His people, praise for all His saints, for the people of Israel who are near to Him.

Sing to the Lord a new song. His praise in the assembly of the faithful! Let Israel be glad in his Maker, let the sons of Zion rejoice in their King!

Let them praise His name with dancing, making melody to Him with timbrel and lyre!

For the Lord takes pleasure in His people; He adorns the humble with victory.

Let the faithful exult in glory; let them sing for joy on their couches. Let the high praises of God be in their throats and two-edged swords in their hands, to wreak vengeance on the nations and chastisement on the peoples, to bind their kings with chains and their nobles with fetters of iron, to execute on them the judgment written! This is glory for all His faithful ones.

Praise God in His sanctuary; praise Him in His mighty firmament!

Praise Him for His mighty deeds; Praise Him according to His exceeding greatness!

Praise Him with trumpet sound; praise Him with lute and harp!

The Praises

A—SHAMED BUT DE—LIV—ERED ME TO DEATH. FORGIVE THEM, O HOLY

FA—THER, FOR THEY KNOW NOT WHAT THEY DO.

Verse: PRAISE HIM WITH TIMBREL AND DANCE; PRAISE HIM WITH STRINGS AND PIPE.

(Repeat) Israel, my first-born son....

Verse: PRAISE HIM WITH SOUNDING CYMBALS; PRAISE HIM WITH LOUD, CLASHING CYMBALS!

Tone 3

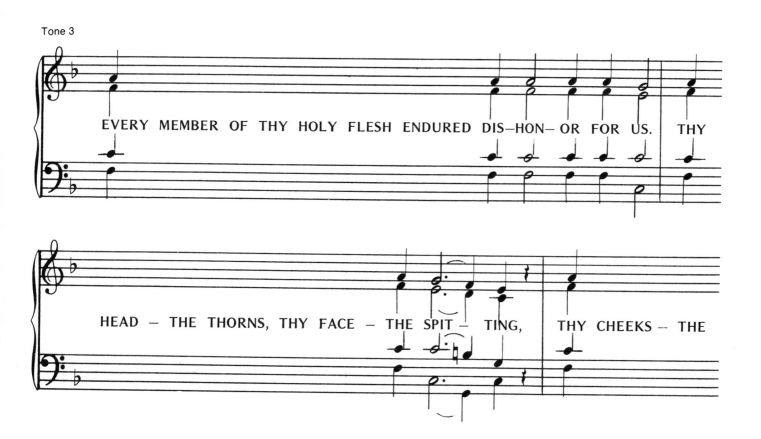

EVERY MEMBER OF THY HOLY FLESH ENDURED DIS—HON—OR FOR US. THY

HEAD — THE THORNS, THY FACE — THE SPIT — TING, THY CHEEKS — THE

THOU DIDST STOOP DOWN TO RAISE US UP. O AL-MIGHTY SA-VIOR,

HAVE MER-CY ON US.

Verse: LET EVERYTHING THAT BREATHES PRAISE THE LORD! PRAISE THE LORD!

Tone 3

BE-HOLD-ING THEE CRU-CI-FIED, O CHRIST, THE WHOLE CREATION TREM-BLED.

THE FOUNDATIONS OF THE EARTH SHOOK FOR FEAR OF THY MIGHT, FOR BY

THY LIFTING UP TODAY THE HEBREW RACE PER-ISHED. THE CURTAIN OF THE

AND BURIED AND RISEN FROM THE DEAD, GLO — RY TO THEE!

(Glory in the 6th Tone) GLORY TO THE FATHER AND TO THE SON AND TO THE HOLY SPIRIT.

Tone 6

THEY HAVE STRIPPED ME OF MY GAR—MENTS AND CLOTHED ME IN A

SCAR—LET ROBE. THEY HAVE SET UPON MY HEAD A CROWN OF THORNS

AND HAVE GIVEN ME A REED IN MY RIGHT HAND THAT I MIGHT DASH

THEM IN PIECES LIKE A POT—TER'S VES — SEL.

(Now and ever in the Same Tone) NOW AND EVER AND UNTO AGES OF AGES.

Tone 6

I GAVE MY BACK TO SCOURG—INGS. I DID NOT TURN MY FACE FROM SPIT — TINGS.

I STOOD BEFORE THE JUDGMENT SEAT OF PI — LATE AND ENDURED THE CROSS

FOR THE SAL—VA—TION OF THE WORLD.

The Praises

Tone 3

A. Kastalsky

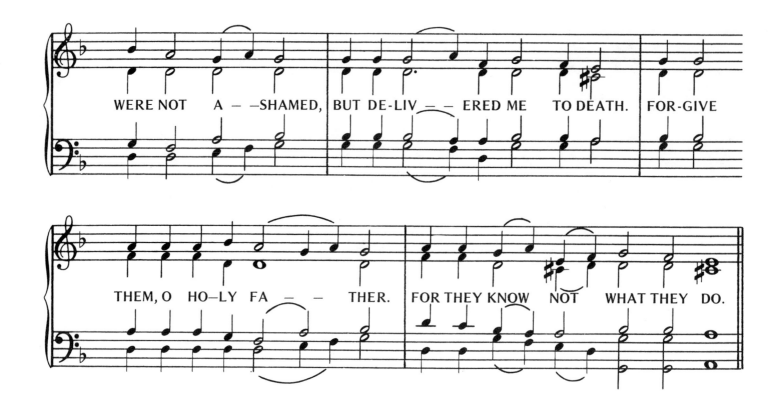

WERE NOT A——SHAMED, BUT DE-LIV——ERED ME TO DEATH. FOR-GIVE

THEM, O HO—LY FA — — THER. FOR THEY KNOW NOT WHAT THEY DO.

Verse: PRAISE HIM WITH TIMBREL AND DANCE; PRAISE HIM WITH STRINGS AND PIPE.

(Repeat) Israel, my first-born son,...

Verse: PRAISE HIM WITH SOUNDING CYMBALS; PRAISE HIM WITH LOUD, CLASHING CYMBALS!

Tone 3

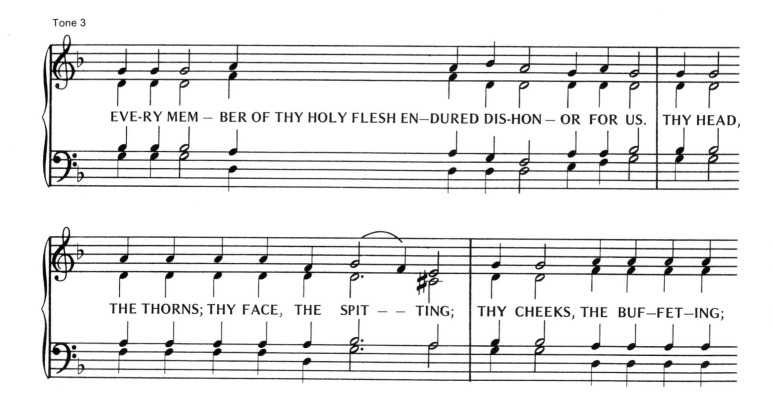

EVE-RY MEM — BER OF THY HOLY FLESH EN—DURED DIS-HON — OR FOR US. THY HEAD,

THE THORNS; THY FACE, THE SPIT — — TING; THY CHEEKS, THE BUF—FET—ING;

Tone 3 *Verse:* LET EVERYTHING THAT BREATHES PRAISE THE LORD! PRAISE THE LORD!

BE—HOLD—ING THEE CRU — CI—FIED, O CHRIST, THE WHOLE CRE—A—TION TREM —

BLED. THE FOUN—DA — TIONS OF THE EARTH SHOOK FOR FEAR OF THY MIGHT,

FOR BY THY LIFT — ING UP TODAY THE HE—BREW RACE PER — —ISHED. THE CUR—

TAIN OF THE TEM—PLE WAS TORN IN TWO. THE TOMBS WERE OPENED AND THE

GLO — RY TO THEE!

(Glory in the 6th Tone)
GLORY TO THE FATHER AND TO THE SON AND TO THE HOLY SPIRIT.

Tone 6

THEY HAVE STRIPPED ME OF MY GAR — MENTS AND CLOTHED ME IN A SCAR —

— LET ROBE. THEY HAVE SET UPON MY HEAD A CROWN OF

THORNS AND HAVE GIVEN ME A REED IN MY RIGHT HAND THAT I MIGHT

DASH THEM IN PIECES LIKE A POT — TER'S VES — — SEL.

(Now and ever in the Same Tone) NOW AND EVER AND UNTO AGES OF AGES.

Tone 6

I GAVE MY BACK TO SCOURG – ING. I DID NOT TURN MY FACE FROM SPIT – – TINGS. I STOOD BEFORE THE JUDGMENT SEAT OF PI – – LATE, AND EN–DURED THE CROSS FOR THE SAL – VA – TION OF THE WORLD!

At the Gospel

The Lesser Doxology

Glory to Thee who hast shown us the light!

Glory to God in the highest, and on earth peace, good will towards men.

We praise Thee! We bless Thee! We worship Thee! We give thanks to Thee for Thy great glory!

O Lord God, heavenly King, God the Father Almighty!

O Lord, the only-begotten Son Jesus Christ, and the Holy Spirit!

O Lord God, Lamb of God, Son of the Father, who takest away the sins of the world, have mercy on us!

Thou that takest away the sins of the world, receive our prayer.

Thou that sittest at the right hand of God the Father, have mercy on us!

For Thou alone art holy, Thou alone art Lord, Thou only, O Jesus Christ, art most high in the glory of God the Father. Amen.

Every day will I give thanks to Thee and praise Thy name forever and ever!

Lord, Thou hast been our refuge from generation to generation!

I said, Lord be merciful to me, heal my soul for I have sinned against Thee. Lord, I flee unto Thee. Teach me to do Thy will, for Thou art my God.

For with Thee is the fountain of life, and in Thy light shall we see light. O continue forth Thy mercy unto those who know Thee!

Vouchsafe, O Lord, to keep us this day without sin. Blessed art Thou, O Lord God of our fathers, and praised and glorified be Thy name forever. Amen.

Let Thy mercy, O Lord be upon us, as we have set our hope on Thee.

Blessed art Thou, O Lord, teach me Thy statutes!

Blessed art Thou, O Master, make me to understand Thy commandments!

Blessed art Thou, O Holy One, enlighten me with Thy precepts!

Thy mercy, O Lord, endures forever, O despise not the works of Thy hands!

To Thee belongs worship! To Thee belongs praise! To Thee belongs glory: to the Father, and to the Son, and to the Holy Spirit, now and ever and unto ages of ages. Amen.

The Litany of Fervent Supplication

Kievan Chant
B. Ledkovsky

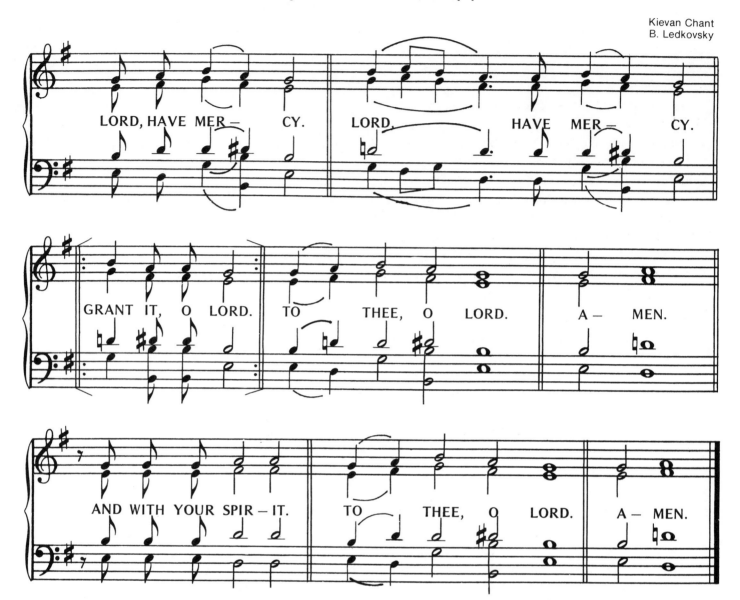

The Litany of Fervent Supplication

S. Glagolev

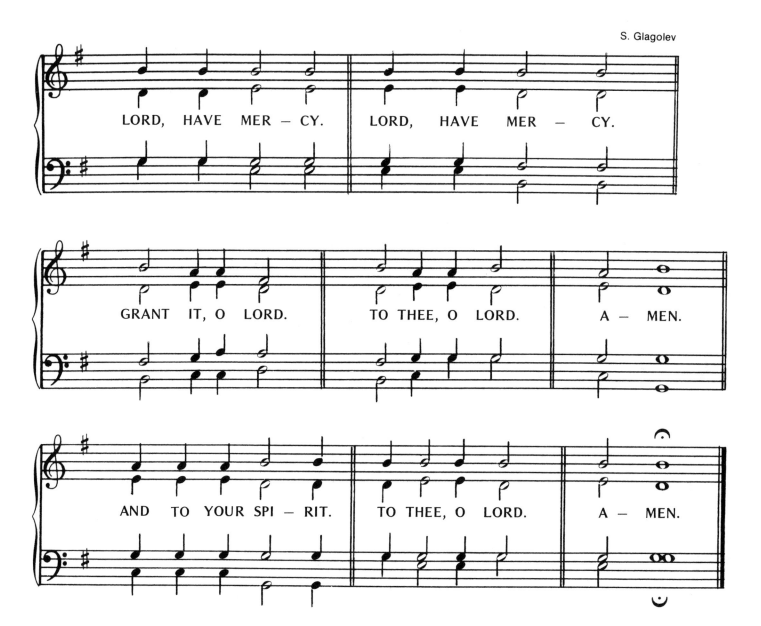

LORD, HAVE MER — CY. LORD, HAVE MER — CY.

GRANT IT, O LORD. TO THEE, O LORD. A — MEN.

AND TO YOUR SPI — RIT. TO THEE, O LORD. A — MEN.

The Litany of Fervent Supplication

Russian Chant

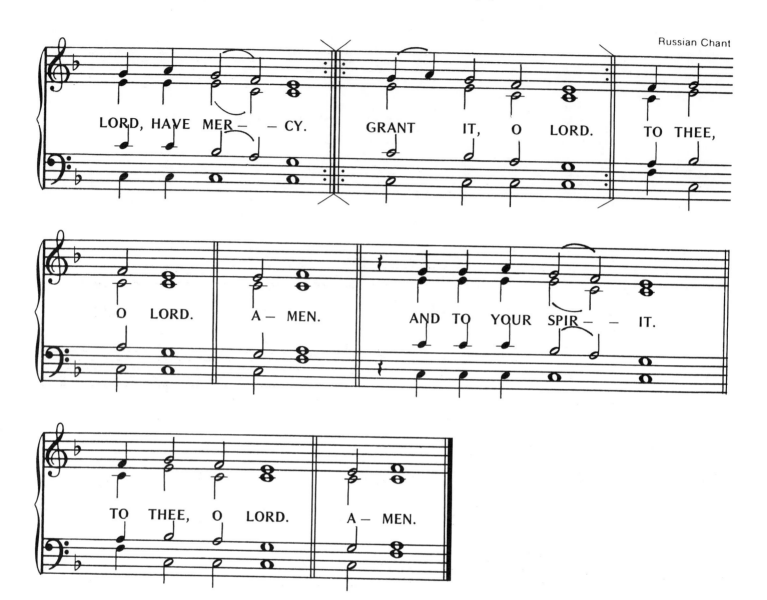

The Litany of Fervent Supplication

Znamenny Chant
A. Arkhangelsky

156

At the Gospel

The Apostikha

Obikhod
N. Bakhmetev

Tone 1

Verse:

THEY DIVIDE MY GARMENTS AMONG THEM, AND FOR MY RAI—MENT, THEY

CAST LOTS.

Tone 2

AN IMPIOUS AND TRANS—GRES—SING PEO — — PLE — WHY DO THEY

IM— AG— INE VAIN THINGS? WHY DO THEY CON—DEMN TO DEATH THE LIFE OF ALL?

O GREAT WON — DER! THE CREATOR OF THE WORLD IS BETRAYED INTO THE

160

CHILD! WOE IS ME, O LIGHT OF THE WORLD! WHY HAST

THOU DEPARTED FROM MINE EYES, O LAMB OF GOD?" THEN THE BODILESS HOSTS

WERE SEIZED WITH TREM — BLING AND CRIED: "O IN—COM—PRE—HEN—SI—BLE

LORD, GLO — RY TO THEE!"

Verse:

GOD IS OUR KING BEFORE THE AGES, HE HAS WROUGHT SALVATION IN THE

AND A—RISE THAT I TOO MAY SEE THY RESURRECTION FROM THE DEAD ON

In the Eighth Tone:

THE THIRD DAY. GLO—RY TO THE FA—THER AND TO THE

SON AND TO THE HO—LY SPIR——IT.

Tone 8

WHEN THOU DIDST AS—CEND THE CROSS, O LORD, FEAR AND TREM—BLING

FELL UP—ON CRE—A————TION, YET THOU DIDST FORBID THE

NOW AND EV—ER AND UN—TO A—GES OF A—GES. A———————MEN.

Tone 8

NOW THE UNJUST JUDGES DIP THE PEN OF JUDG——MENT. JE—SUS

IS TRIED AND SEN—TENCED TO THE CROSS. ALL CREATION SUFFERS AS IT

BE—HOLDS THE LORD ON THE CROSS. O GOOD LORD, WHO IN THY

HU—MAN NATURE DIDST SUFFER FOR ME, GLO—RY TO THEE!

The Apostikha

Tone 1

Kievan Chant
A. Kastalsky

ALL CRE – A — — — TION WAS CHANGED BY FEAR WHEN IT SAW THEE

HANG—ING UP —ON THE CROSS, O CHRIST. THE SUN WAS DARK —

ENED, AND THE FOUNDATIONS OF THE EARTH WERE SHAK — — — EN.

ALL THINGS SUF — — FERED WITH THE CRE – A –TOR OF ALL O LORD,

WHO DIDST WILLINGLY ENDURE THIS FOR US, GLO — RY TO THEE !

Verse: They divide my garments among them, and for my raiment, they cast lots.

Tone 2

AN IM — — PI—OUS AND TRANS—GRES—SING PEO — PLE WHY DO THEY IM — AG — INE VAIN THINGS? WHY DO THEY CONDEMN TO DEATH THE LIFE OF ALL? O GREAT WON — — — DER! THE CREATOR OF THE WORLD IS BETRAYED INTO THE HANDS OF LAW — — LESS MEN. HE WHO LOVES MANKIND IS LIFTED UP UP — ON THE WOOD THAT HE MIGHT FREE

THOSE BOUND IN HELL WHO CRY: O LONG—SUF—FER—ING LORD

GLO — RY TO THEE!

Verse: They gave me gall for food, and for my thirst
they gave me vinegar to drink.

Tone 2

TO — DAY THE BLAME—LESS VIR — GIN SAW THEE SUSPENDED UP—ON THE

CROSS, O WORD. SHE MOURNED WITH—IN HERSELF AND WAS SORE—LY

PIERCED IN HER HEART. SHE GROANED IN AG—O—NY FROM THE DEPTH OF

O IN—COM—PRE—HEN—SI—BLE LORD, GLO — RY TO THEE!

Tone 2

Verse: God is our King before the ages: He has wrought salvation in the midst of the earth.

WHEN SHE WHO BORE THEE WITH—OUT SEED SAW THEE SUS —

—PEND—ED UP — ON THE TREE, O CHRIST, THE CRE — A — TOR

AND GOD OF ALL, SHE CRIED BIT — TER — LY: WHERE IS THE BEAUTY OF

THY FORM, O MY SON? I CANNOT BEAR TO SEE THEE UN—JUST—LY

CRU – – CI – FIED. HAS – TEN AND A – RISE, THAT I

TOO MAY SEE THY RESURRECTION FROM THE DEAD ON THE THIRD DAY.

(Glory in the 8th Tone) **Glory to the Father and to the Son and to the Holy Spirit.**

Tone 8

Kievan Chant

WHEN THOU DIDST AS – CEND THE CROSS, O LORD, FEAR AND TREM – BLING

FELL UP – ON CRE – A – – – TION, YET THOU DIDST FORBID THE

EARTH TO SWAL – LOW UP THOSE WHO CRU – CI – FIED THEE,

AND THOU DIDST COMMAND HELL TO SEND UP ITS CAP — — TIVES FOR THE

RE — GEN — ER — A — TION OF MOR — — — TALS. O JUDGE OF THE

LIV — ING AND THE DEAD: THOU HAST COME TO GRANT LIFE

NOT DEATH. O LOV — ER OF MAN — KIND, GLO — RY TO THEE!

(Now and ever in the Same Tone) Now and ever and unto ages of ages. Amen.

Tone 8

NOW THE UNJUST JUDGES DIP THE PEN OF JUDG — — MENT. JE — SUS

IS TRIED AND SEN — TENCED TO THE CROSS. ALL CREATION SUFFERS AS IT

BE—HOLDS THE LORD ON THE CROSS. O GOOD LORD, WHO IN

THY HUMAN NATURE DIDST SUFFER FOR ME, GLO — RY TO THEE !

At the Gospel

Kievan

Priest: That we may be accounted worthy...

LORD, HAVE MER—CY, LORD, HAVE MER—CY, LORD, HAVE MER — CY,

Priest: Wisdom!...Peace be unto all!

AND TO YOUR SPIR — — IT.

Before the Gospel:

GLO — RY TO THY PAS—SION O LORD, O LORD.

After the Gospel:

GLO — RY TO THY LONG-SUF—FER—ING O LORD,

O LORD.

The Trisagion Prayers

READER:

It is good to give thanks to the Lord, to sing praises to Thy name, O Most high;
to declare Thy mercy in the morning, and Thy truth by night.

Holy God, Holy Mighty, Holy Immortal, have mercy on us!
Holy God, Holy Mighty, Holy Immortal, have mercy on us!
Holy God, Holy Mighty, Holy Immortal, have mercy on us!

Glory to the Father, and to the Son, and to the Holy Spirit, now and ever and unto
ages of ages. Amen.

O Most-holy Trinity: have mercy on us.
O Lord: cleanse us from our sins.
O Master: pardon our transgressions.
O Holy One: visit and heal our infirmities, for Thy name's sake.

Lord, have mercy. Lord, have mercy. Lord, have mercy.

Glory to the Father, and to the Son, and to the Holy Spirit, now and ever and unto
ages of ages. Amen.

Our Father, who art in heaven, hallowed be Thy name. Thy Kingdom come. Thy will be done,
on earth as it is in heaven. Give us this day our daily bread; and forgive us our trespasses, as
we forgive those who trespass against us; and lead us not into temptation, but deliver us from
evil.

The Troparion

Tone 4

D. Yaichkov

BY THY PRE – CIOUS BLOOD THOU HAST RE–DEEMED US FROM THE

CURSE OF THE LAW. BY BEING NAILED TO THE CROSS AND PIERCED

BY A SPEAR THOU HAST POURED FORTH IM – MOR–TAL – I – TY

FOR MAN. O OUR SAV–IOR, GLO – RY TO THEE.

The Troparion

Tone 4

Kievan Chant

The Augmented Litany

Kievan Chant
B. Ledkovskoy

The Augmented Litany

S. Glagolev

The Augmented Litany

Russian Chant

LORD, HAVE MER—CY. LORD, HAVE MERCY. LORD, HAVE MER — —CY. A— MEN.

The Augmented Litany

Znamenny Chant
A. Arkhangelsky

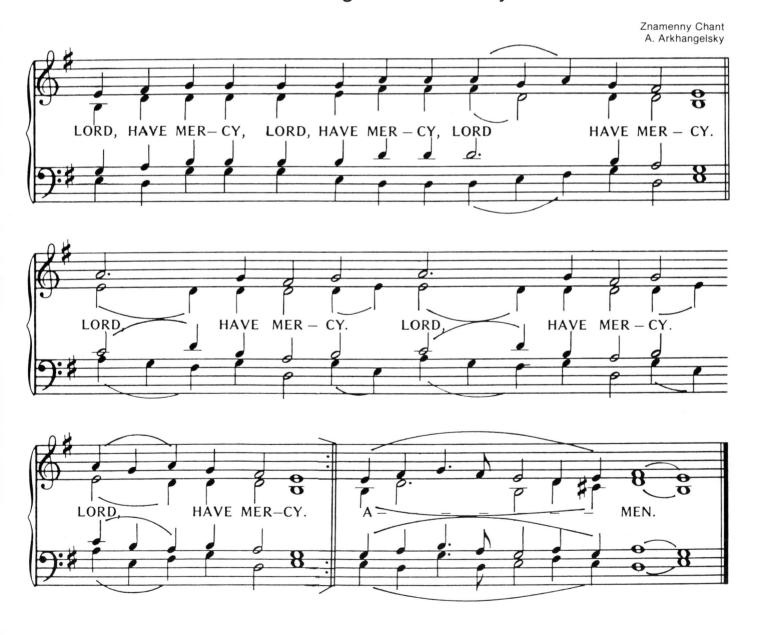

LORD, HAVE MER—CY, LORD, HAVE MER—CY, LORD HAVE MER—CY.

LORD, HAVE MER—CY. LORD, HAVE MER—CY.

LORD, HAVE MER—CY. A— MEN.

The Augmented Litany

Byzantine Chant

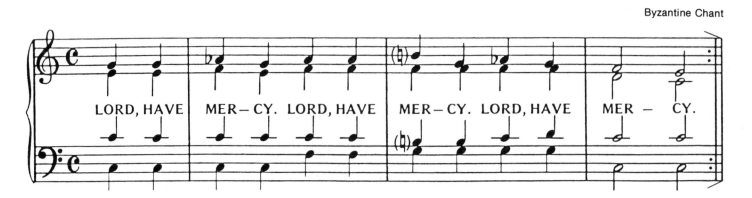

LORD, HAVE MER—CY. LORD, HAVE MER—CY. LORD, HAVE MER — CY.

A — MEN.

The Augmented Litany

Kievan Chant

1 LORD, HAVE MERCY, LORD, HAVE MER — CY, LORD, HAVE MER — CY.

2 LORD, HAVE MER-CY, LORD, HAVE MER-CY, LORD, HAVE MER — CY. A — MEN.

The Great Dismissal

B. Ledkovsky

The Royal Hours

The First Hour

THE TROPARION (Tone 1)

THE TYRANT HAS BEEN DESTROYED BY THY CRUCIFIXION, O CHRIST
THE MIGHT OF THE ENEMY HAS BEEN TRAMPLED DOWN.
FOR NEITHER AN ANGEL NOR A MAN
BUT THOU THYSELF HAST SAVE US.
O LORD, GLORY TO THEE!

STIKHERA (Tone 8)

(cf. p. 74 for musical setting)
TODAY THE CURTAIN OF THE TEMPLE IS TORN IN TWO,
TO CONVICT THE TRANSGRESSORS,
AND EVEN THE SUN HIDES HIS RAYS,
SEEING THE MASTER CRUCIFIED.

Verse: Why do the nations rage and the peoples utter folly?

THOU WAST LED AS A SHEEP TO THE SLAUGHTER, O CHRIST OUR KING,
AND AS AN INNOCENT LAMB,
THOU WAST NAILED TO THE CROSS BY TRANSGRESSORS,
BECAUSE OF OUR SINS, O LOVER OF MANKIND!

Verse: The kings of the earth rise up, and the rulers take counsel together, against the Lord and His anointed.

THOU WAST LED . . . .

Verse: Glory to the Father and to the Son and to the Holy Spirit.

(cf. p. 55 for musical setting)
WHILE PERMITTING TRANSGRESSORS TO ARREST THEE,
THOU DIDST CRY OUT TO THEM, O LORD:
THOUGH YOU SMITE THE SHEPHERD AND SCATTER THE TWELVE SHEEP, MY DISCIPLES,
I AM ABLE TO SURROUND MYSELF WITH MORE THAN THIRTY LEGIONS OF ANGELS,
BUT I FOREBEAR,
SO THAT THE SECRET AND HIDDEN THINGS MIGHT BE FULFILLED,
WHICH WERE REVEALED TO YOU BY MY PROPHETS.
O LORD, GLORY TO THEE!

Verse: Now and ever and unto ages of ages. Amen.

WHILE PERMITTING . . . .

The Prokeimenon of the Prophecy

Tone 4

Znamenny Chant
A. Arkhangelsky

Psalm 41

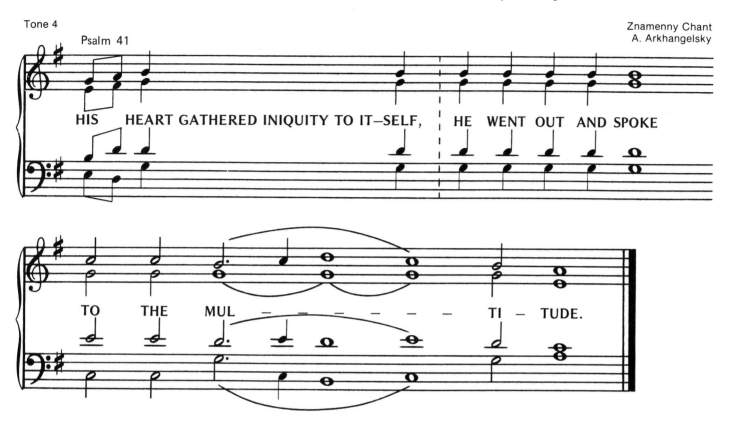

HIS HEART GATHERED INIQUITY TO IT—SELF, HE WENT OUT AND SPOKE

TO THE MUL — — — — — — TI — TUDE.

Verse: **BLESSED IS HE WHO CONSIDERS THE POOR AND NEEDY; THE LORD DELIVERS HIM
IN THE DAY OF TROUBLE.**

The Third Hour

THE TROPARION (Tone 6)

O LORD, THE LIFE OF ALL,
THE JEWS DELIVERED THEE OVER TO DEATH.
THOU DIDST LEAD THEM THROUGH THE RED SEA BY MOSES' ROD,
YET THEY HANDED THEE OVER TO BE CRUCIFIED.
THOU DIDST FEED THEM WITH HONEY FROM THE ROCK,
AND THEY REPAID THEE WITH GALL AND VINEGAR,
BUT THOU DIDST WILLINGLY ENDURE THESE THINGS,
TO FREE US FROM BONDAGE TO THE ENEMY.
O CHRIST GOD, GLORY TO THEE!

STIKHERA (Tone 8)

FOR FEAR OF THE JEWS, O LORD.
THY FRIEND AND COMPANION PETER DENIED THEE.
IN BITTER GRIEF, HE CRIED ALOUD:
"O COMPASSIONATE MASTER,
TURN NOT AWAY IN SILENCE FROM MY TEARS.
I SAID THAT I WOULD KEEP FAITH, BUT HAVE FAILED THEE."
ACCEPT ALSO OUR REPENTANCE AND HAVE MERCY ON US, O LORD!

Verse: Give ear to my words, O Lord; give heed to my groaning.

BEFORE THY CRUCIFIXION, O LORD,
AS THE SOLDIERS WERE MOCKING THEE,
THE ANGELS HID THEIR FACES, UNABLE TO BEAR THE SIGHT,
FOR THOU WHO DIDST ADORN THE EARTH WITH FLOWERS
WAST ARRAYED IN A CROWN OF THORNS;
THOU WHO HAST WRAPPED THE HEAVENS WITH CLOUDS
WAST CLOTHED IN A ROBE OF MOCKERY,
YET ALL THESE THINGS FULFILLED THY SAVING PLAN,
BY WHICH THY COMPASSION WAS REVEALED TO US.
O CHRIST OF GREAT MERCY, GLORY TO THEE!

Verse: Hearken to the sound of my cry, my King and my God.

BEFORE THY CRUCIFIXION . . . .

Verse: (In the 5th Tone) Glory to the Father and to the Son and to the Holy Spirit.

(Tone 5)

WHEN THOU WAST RAISED UPON THE CROSS, O LORD,
THOU DIDST CRY OUT TO THE JEWS:
FOR WHAT DEEDS DO YOU CRUCIFY ME, O MY PEOPLE?
IS IT BECAUSE I MADE YOUR PARALYTICS WALK?
BECAUSE I RAISED THE DEAD AS FROM SLEEP?
BECAUSE I HEALED THE WOMAN WITH THE ISSUE OF BLOOD,
AND TOOK PITY ON THE WOMAN OF CANAAN?
FOR WHAT DEEDS DO YOU SEEK TO KILL ME?
YOU SHALL LOOK UPON HIM WHOM YOU HAVE PIERCED,
UPON YOUR MESSIAH, O TRANSGRESSORS.

Verse: Now and ever and unto ages of ages. Amen.

WHEN THOU WAST RAISED . . . .

The Prokeimenon of the Prophecy

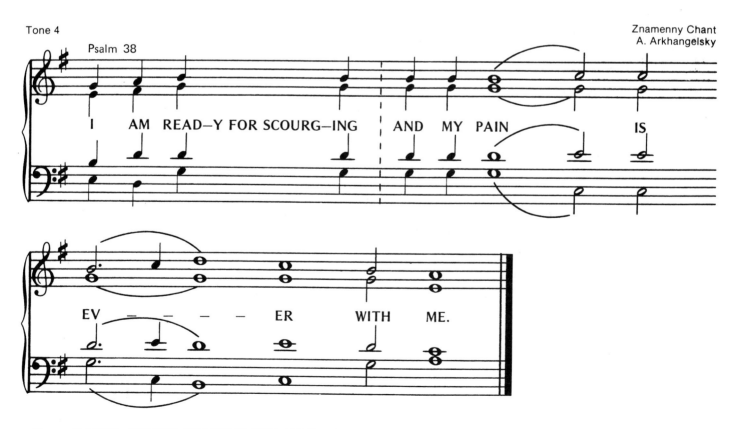

Tone 4

Psalm 38

Znamenny Chant
A. Arkhangelsky

I AM READ—Y FOR SCOURG—ING AND MY PAIN IS EV — — — — ER WITH ME.

Verse: O LORD, REBUKE ME NOT IN THY ANGER, NOR CHASTEN ME IN THY WRATH.

The Sixth Hour

THE TROPARION (Tone 2)

THOU HAST WORKED SALVATION IN THE MIDST OF THE EARTH, O CHRIST OUR GOD;
BY STRETCHING OUT THY MOST PURE HANDS UPON THE CROSS.
GATHERING TOGETHER ALL THE NATIONS, WHO CRY:
O LORD, GLORY TO THEE!

STIKHERA (Tone 8)

(cf. p. 73 for musical setting)
THUS SAYS THE LORD TO THE JEWS:
MY PEOPLE, WHAT HAVE I DONE TO YOU,
OR HOW HAVE I OFFENDED YOU?
TO YOUR BLIND I GAVE SIGHT, YOUR LEPERS I CLEANSED,
THE PARALYTIC I RAISED FROM HIS BED.
MY PEOPLE, WHAT HAVE I DONE TO YOU,
AND HOW HAVE YOU REPAID ME?
INSTEAD OF MANNA, GALL; INSTEAD OF WATER, VINEGAR;
INSTEAD OF LOVING ME, YOU NAIL ME TO THE CROSS.
I CAN BEAR NO MORE.
I SHALL CALL THE GENTILES MINE.
THEY WILL GLORIFY ME WITH THE FATHER AND THE SPIRIT,
AND I SHALL GIVE THEM LIFE ETERNAL.

Verse: They gave me gall for food, and in my thirst they gave me vinegar to drink.

(cf. p. 75 for musical setting)
THE CHOIR OF THE APOSTLES CRIES OUT TO YOU,
O LAW-GIVERS OF ISRAEL, SCRIBES AND PHRAISEES;
BEHOLD THE TEMPLE WHICH YOU DESTROYED!
BEHOLD THE LAMB WHOM YOU CRUCIFIED!
YOU DELIVERED HIM TO THE TOMB, BUT BY HIS OWN POWER HE AROSE.
DO NOT BE DECEIVED, O JEWS.
HE IT IS THAT SAVED YOU IN THE SEA AND FED YOU IN THE WILDERNESS.
HE IS THE LIFE, THE LIGHT, AND THE PEACE OF THE WORLD.

Verse: Save me, O God, for the waters have come up to my neck.

THE CHOIR OF THE APOSTLES . . . .

Verse: (In the 5th Tone) Glory to the Father and to the Son and to the Holy Spirit.

(Tone 5)

COME, O CHRIST-BEARING PEOPLE!
LET US SEE WHAT THE TRAITOR JUDAS AND THE LAWLESS PRIESTS
HAVE PLOTTED AGAINST OUR SAVIOR.
TODAY THEY MADE THE DEATHLESS WORD SUBJECT TO DEATH.
THEY DELIVERED HIM TO PILATE
AND CRUCIFIED HIM ON GOLGOTHA.
SUFFERING THESE THINGS OUR SAVIOR CRIED ALOUD AND SAID:
"FATHER, FORGIVE THEM THIS SIN,
THAT ALL NATIONS MAY KNOW MY RESURRECTION FROM THE DEAD."

Verse: Now and ever and unto ages of ages. Amen.

COME, O CHRIST-BEARING PEOPLE . . . .

The Prokeimenon of the Prophecy

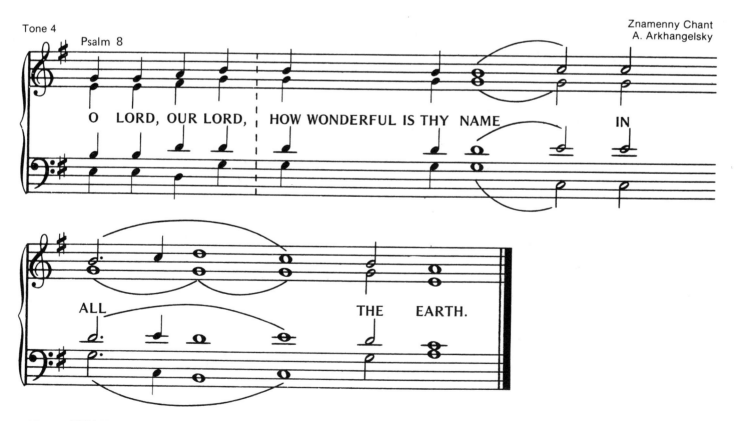

Verse: THY MAJESTY IS EXALTED ABOVE THE HEAVENS.

The Ninth Hour

THE TROPARION (Tone 8)

WHEN THE THIEF BEHELD THE AUTHOR OF LIFE HANGING UPON THE CROSS, HE SAID:
"IF IT WERE NOT GOD IN THE FLESH CRUCIFIED HERE WITH US,
THE SUN WOULD NOT HAVE HIDDEN HIS RAYS NOR WOULD THE EARTH HAVE
    QUAKED AND TREMBLED,
BUT REMEMBER ME IN THY KINGDOM, O LONG-SUFFERING LORD!"

STIKHERA (Tone 7)

A STRANGE WONDER IT WAS TO SEE THE MAKER OF HEAVEN AND EARTH SUSPENDED
    ON THE CROSS.
THE SUN WAS DARKENED AND THE DAY WAS CHANGED INTO NIGHT.
THE EARTH GAVE UP THE BODIES OF THE DEAD FROM THEIR GRAVES.
WITH THEM WE WORSHIP THEE: SAVE US, O LORD!

Verse: They divide my garments among them, and for my raiment they cast lots.

(Tone 2)
WHEN TRANSGRESSORS NAILED THE KING OF GLORY TO THE CROSS,
HE CRIED OUT TO THEM:
"HOW HAVE I CAUSED YOU PAIN?
OR IN WHAT HAVE I ANGERED YOU?
WHO BEFORE ME DELIVERED YOU FROM AFFLICTION?
AND HOW HAVE YOU NOW REWARDED ME?
BY RETURNING EVIL FOR GOOD.
FOR THE PILLAR OF FIRE YOU NAIL ME TO THE CROSS.
FOR THE CLOUD YOU DIG ME A GRAVE.
INSTEAD OF MANNA YOU BRING ME GALL.
INSTEAD OF WATER YOU GIVE ME VINEGAR TO DRINK.
HENCEFORTH I SHALL CALL THE GENTILES,
AND THEY WILL GLORIFY ME WITH THE FATHER AND THE HOLY SPIRIT."

Verse: They gave me gall for food and in my thirst they gave me vinegar to drink.

WHEN TRANSGRESSORS . . . .

Verse: (In the 6th Tone) Glory to the Father and to the Son and to the Holy Spirit, now and ever and unto ages of ages. Amen.

(Tone 6 — cf. p. 85f. for musical settings)

TODAY HE WHO HUNG THE EARTH UPON THE WATERS IS HUNG ON THE TREE.

THE KING OF THE ANGELS IS DECKED WITH A CROWN OF THORNS.

HE WHO WRAPS THE HEAVENS IN CLOUDS IS WRAPPED IN THE PURPLE OF MOCKERY.

HE WHO FREED ADAM IN THE JORDAN IS SLAPPED ON THE FACE.

THE BRIDEGROOM OF THE CHURCH IS AFFIXED TO THE CROSS WITH NAILS.

THE SON OF THE VIRGIN IS PIERCED BY A SPEAR.

WE WORSHIP THY PASSION, O CHRIST.

WE WORSHIP THY PASSION, O CHRIST.

WE WORSHIP THY PASSION, O CHRIST.

SHOW US ALSO THY GLORIOUS RESURRECTION.

The Prokeimenon of the Prophecy

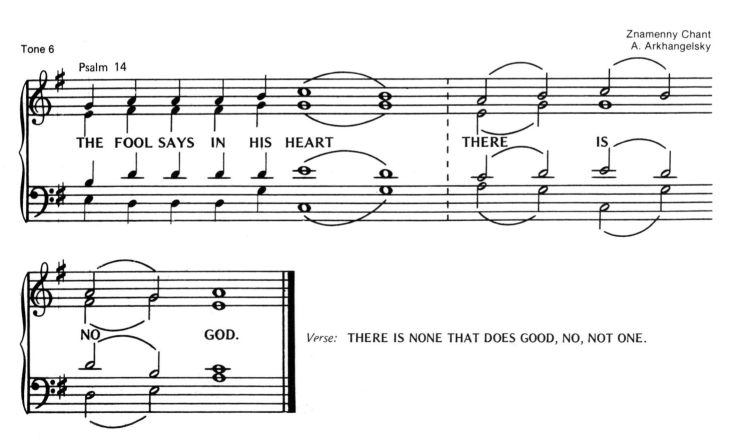

Znamenny Chant
A. Arkhangelsky

Tone 6

Psalm 14

THE FOOL SAYS IN HIS HEART THERE IS NO GOD.

Verse: THERE IS NONE THAT DOES GOOD, NO, NOT ONE.

Vespers

The Great Litany

Kievan Chant
B. Ledkovsky

The Great Litany

Carpatho-Russian

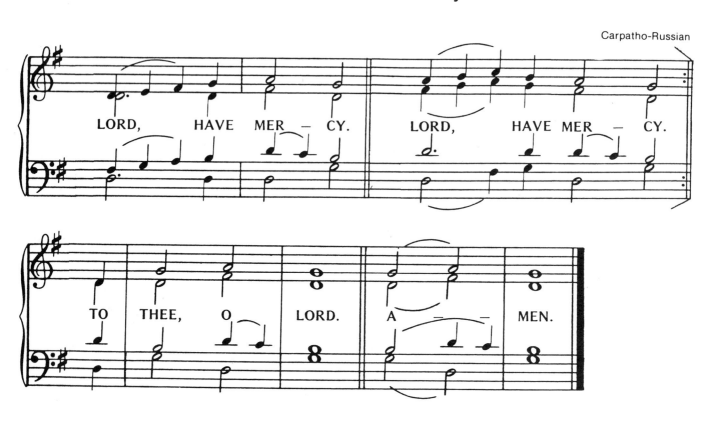

The Great Litany

Byzantine Chant

The Great Litany

Russian Chant

LORD, HAVE MER—CY.   TO THEE, O LORD   A—MEN.

The Great Litany

Znamenny Chant
A. Arkhangelsky

LORD, HAVE MER—CY.   TO THEE,   O   LORD.   A—MEN.

Lord, I Call Upon Thee

Obikhod
N. Bakhmetev

Tone 1

Set a guard over my mouth, O Lord, keep watch over the door of my lips!

Incline not my heart to any evil, to busy myself with wicked deeds in company with men who work iniquity, and let me not partake of their delights!

Let a good man strike or rebuke me in kindness, but let the oil of the wicked never anoint my head for my prayer is continually against their wicked deeds.

When they are given over to those who shall condemn them, then they shall learn that the word of the Lord is true.

As a rock which one cleaves and shatters on the land, so shall their bones be strewn at the mouth of Sheol.

But my eyes are toward Thee, O Lord God; in Thee I seek refuge; leave me not defenseless!

Keep me from the trap which they have laid for me, and from the snares of evildoers!

Let the wicked together fall into their own nets, while I escape.

I cry with my voice to the Lord, with my voice I make supplication to the Lord, I pour out my trouble before Him.

When my spirit departs from me, Thou knowest my way!

In the path where I walk they have hidden a trap for me.

I look to the right and watch, but there is none who takes notice of me; no refuge remains to me, no man cares for me.

I cry to Thee, O Lord; I say Thou art my refuge, my portion in the land of the living.

Give heed to my cry; for I am brought very low!

Deliver me from my persecutors; for they are too strong for me!

Bring my soul out of prison, that I may give thanks to Thy name.

The righteous will surround me, for Thou wilt deal bountifully with me.

Out of the depths I cry to Thee, O Lord! Lord, hear my voice!

Let Thine ears be attentive to the voice of my supplications.

If Thou, O Lord, shouldst mark iniquities, Lord, who could stand? But there is forgiveness with Thee.

Tone 1

Obikhod
N. Bakhmetev

ALL CRE – A – TION WAS CHANGED BY FEAR WHEN IT SAW THEE HANG–ING

UP – ON THE CROSS, O CHRIST. THE SUN WAS DARK–ENED, AND THE

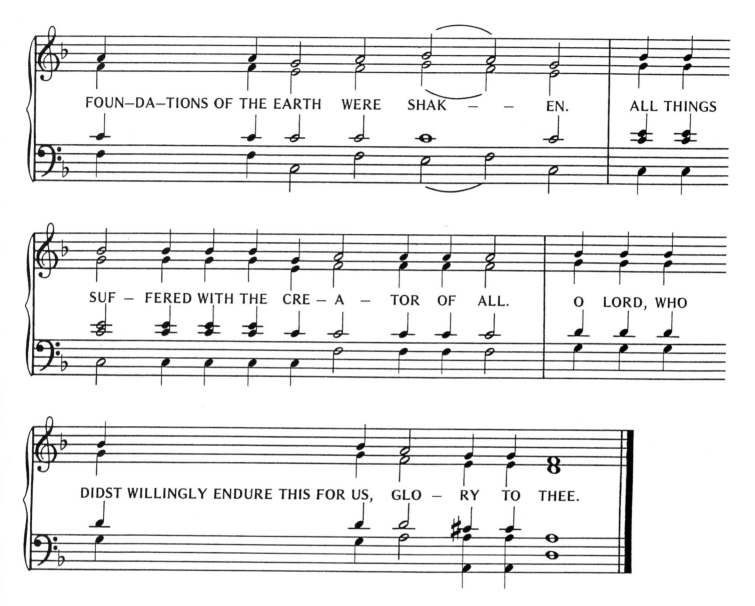

FOUN–DA–TIONS OF THE EARTH WERE SHAK — — EN. ALL THINGS

SUF — FERED WITH THE CRE — A — TOR OF ALL. O LORD, WHO

DIDST WILLINGLY ENDURE THIS FOR US, GLO — RY TO THEE.

Verse: FOR THY NAME'S SAKE I WAIT FOR THEE, O LORD; MY SOUL HAS WAITED FOR THY WORD; MY SOUL HAS HOPED ON THE LORD.

(Repeat): All creation was changed...

Verse: FROM THE MORNING WATCH UNTIL NIGHT, FROM THE MORNING WATCH, LET ISRAEL HOPE ON THE LORD.

Tone 2

AN IMPIOUS AND TRANS–GRES–SING PEO — — PLE — WHY DO THEY

Verse: PRAISE THE LORD, ALL NATIONS! PRAISE HIM ALL PEOPLES!

THE THIRD DAY.

Verse: FOR HIS MERCY IS CONFIRMED ON US, AND THE TRUTH OF THE LORD ENDURES FOREVER.

Tone 6

TO—DAY THE MASTER OF CREATION STANDS BE—FORE PI — LATE. TO — DAY

THE CREATOR OF ALL IS CONDEMNED TO DIE ON THE CROSS. OF HIS

OWN WILL, HE IS LED AS A LAMB TO THE SLAUGH — TER. HE WHO FED HIS

PEO—PLE WITH MANNA IN THE DESERT IS TRANS-FIXED WITH NAILS. HIS SIDE IS

206

Verse: GLORY TO THE FATHER, AND TO THE SON, AND TO THE HOLY SPIRIT.

Tone 6

SEE HOW THE LAWLESS ASSEMBLY CONDEMNS THE KING OF CRE — A — TION TO DEATH.

THEY ARE NOT ASHAMED, EVEN WHEN HE REMINDS THEM OF HIS MIGHT — Y WORKS:

"MY PEOPLE, WHAT HAVE I DONE TO YOU? HAVE I NOT FILLED JU—DE—A

WITH MIR — A — CLES? HAVE I NOT RAISED THE DEAD BY MY WORD A — LONE?

HAVE I NOT HEALED EVE—RY SICK — NESS AND DIS — EASE? HOW HAVE YOU

GLO — RY TO THEE!

Verse: NOW AND EVER, AND UNTO AGES OF AGES. AMEN.

Tone 6

WE SEE A STRANGE AND FEARFUL MYSTERY AC—COM-PLISHED TO— DAY. HE WHOM

NONE MAY TOUCH IS SEIZED. HE WHO LOOSES ADAM FROM THE CURSE

IS BOUND. HE WHO TRIES THE HEARTS OF MEN IS UN—JUST—LY BROUGHT

TO TRIAL. HE WHO CLOSED THE ABYSS IS SHUT IN PRIS — — ON.

ALL MEN FROM THE CURSE. O LONG—SUFFERING LORD, GLO — RY TO THEE!

Lord, I Call Upon Thee

Kievan Chant
B. Ledkovsky

Tone 1

LORD, I CALL UPON THEE, HEAR ME. HEAR ME, O LORD. LORD, I CALL

UP—ON THEE, HEAR ME, RE—CEIVE THE VOICE OF MY PRAYER WHEN I

CALL UP—ON THEE, HEAR ME, O LORD. LET MY PRAYER A—

—RISE IN THY SIGHT AS IN—CENSE, AND LET THE LIFT—ING UP OF MY

HANDS BE AN EVE—NING SA—CRI—FICE. HEAR ME, O LORD.

Set a guard over my mouth, O Lord, keep watch over the door of my lips!

Incline not my heart to any evil, to busy myself with wicked deeds in company with men who work iniquity, and let me not partake of their delights!

Let a good man strike or rebuke me in kindness, but let the oil of the wicked never anoint my head for my prayer is continually against their wicked deeds.

When they are given over to those who shall condemn them, then they shall learn that the word of the Lord is true.

As a rock which one cleaves and shatters on the land, so shall their bones be strewn at the mouth of Sheol.

But my eyes are toward Thee, O Lord God; in Thee I seek refuge; leave me not defenseless!

Keep me from the trap which they have laid for me, and from the snares of evildoers!

Let the wicked together fall into their own nets, while I escape.

I cry with my voice to the Lord, with my voice I make supplication to the Lord, I pour out my trouble before Him.

When my spirit departs from me, Thou knowest my way!

In the path where I walk they have hidden a trap for me.

I look to the right and watch, but there is none who takes notice of me; no refuge remains to me, no man cares for me.

I cry to Thee, O Lord; I say Thou art my refuge, my portion in the land of the living.

Give heed to my cry; for I am brought very low!

Deliver me from my persecutors; for they are too strong for me!

Bring my soul out of prison, that I may give thanks to Thy name.

The righteous will surround me, for Thou wilt deal bountifully with me.

Out of the depths I cry to Thee, O Lord! Lord, hear my voice!

Let Thine ears be attentive to the voice of my supplications.

Tone 1

ALL CRE-A — — TION WAS CHANGED BY FEAR WHEN IT SAW THEE

HANG—ING ON THE CROSS, O CHRIST! THE SUN WAS DARK-ENED,

AND THE FOUNDATIONS OF THE EARTH WERE SHAK — — EN. ALL THINGS

SUF — — FERED WITH THE CRE-A-TOR OF ALL. O LORD, WHO

DIDST WILLINGLY ENDURE THIS FOR US, GLO — — RY TO THEE!

214

FOR THY NAME'S SAKE I WAIT FOR THEE, O LORD. MY SOUL HAS WAITED

FOR THY WORD, MY SOUL HAS HOPED ON THE LORD.

(Repeat) ALL CREATION WAS CHANGED . . .

In the 2nd Tone:

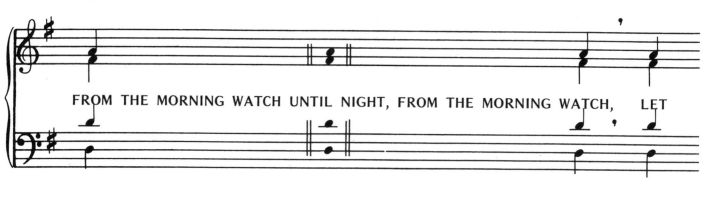

FROM THE MORNING WATCH UNTIL NIGHT, FROM THE MORNING WATCH, LET

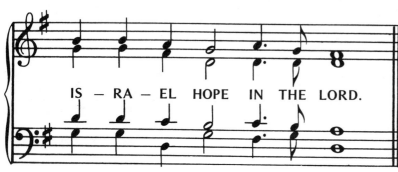

IS — RA — EL HOPE IN THE LORD.

Tone 2

FREE THOSE BOUND IN HELL, WHO CRY: O LONG—SUF—FER—ING

LORD, GLO — RY TO THEE!

FOR WITH THE LORD THERE IS MERCY AND WITH HIM IS REDEMPTION AND

HE WILL DELIVER ISRAEL FROM ALL HIS IN—I — QUI — TIES.

Tone 2

TO — DAY THE BLAME—LESS VIR — GIN SAW THEE SUSPENDED UP—ON

Tone 2

FROM THE DEAD ON THE THIRD DAY."

In the 6th Tone:

FOR HIS MERCY IS CONFIRMED ON US, AND THE TRUTH OF THE LORD

EN — DURES FOR — E — VER!

Tone 6

TO—DAY THE MASTER OF CREATION STANDS BE—FORE PI — LATE. TO—DAY

THE CREATOR OF ALL IS CONDEMNED TO DIE ON THE CROSS. OF HIS OWN

MAN—KIND! FOR THOSE WHO CRU—CI—FIED HIM, HE PRAYED TO HIS FA—THER

SAY — — — ING: "FOR — GIVE THEM THIS SIN, FOR THEY KNOW

NOT WHAT THEY DO." GLO—RY TO THE FATHER AND TO THE SON AND

TO THE HO — — — — —LY SPIR — — — —IT.

Tone 6

SEE HOW THE LAWLESS ASSEMBLY CONDEMNS THE KING OF CRE — A — — TION TO

DEATH. THEY ARE NOT ASHAMED, EVEN WHEN HE REMINDS THEM OF HIS MIGHT—Y

WORKS: "MY PEO— PLE, WHAT HAVE I DONE TO YOU?

HAVE I NOT FILLED JU—DE—A WITH MIR — A — CLES? HAVE I NOT RAISED THE

DEAD BY MY WORD A — LONE? HAVE I NOT HEALED EVE—RY SICK—NESS

AND DIS—EASE? HOW HAVE YOU RE—PAID ME? WHY HAVE YOU

Tone 6

O Gladsome Light

Abbreviated Kievan Chant
B. Ledkovsky

O GLAD—SOME LIGHT OF THE HO—LY GLO—RY OF THE IM—

MOR—TAL FA—THER, HEA—VEN—LY, HO—LY, BLESS—

ED JE—SUS CHRIST, NOW THAT WE HAVE COME TO

THE SET—TING OF THE SUN, AND BE—HOLD THE LIGHT OF

EVE—NING, WE PRAISE GOD, FA—THER, SON, AND HO—LY

SPIR — —IT. FOR MEET IT IS AT ALL

TIMES TO WOR — SHIP THEE WITH VOIC — ES OF PRAISE, O SON

OF GOD AND GIV — ER OF LIFE: THERE — FORE ALL

THE WORLD DOTH GLO — RI — FY THEE.

O Gladsome Light

Kievan Chant
B. Ledkovsky

O Gladsome Light

Greek Melody

O GLAD—SOME LIGHT OF THE HO-LY GLO——RY

OF TH'IM—MOR—TAL FA——THER, HEAV—EN—LY, HO——LY,

BLESS——ED JE——SUS CHRIST:

NOW THAT WE HAVE COME TO THE SET—TING OF THE SUN

AND BE-HOLD THE LIGHT OF EVE——NING WE PRAISE GOD,

O Gladsome Light

Kievan Chant
Arch. Theofan

O Gladsome Light

SON OF GOD AND GIV — —ER OF LIFE.

THERE — FORE ALL THE WORLD DOTH GLO —RI—FY THEE.

The First Prokeimenon

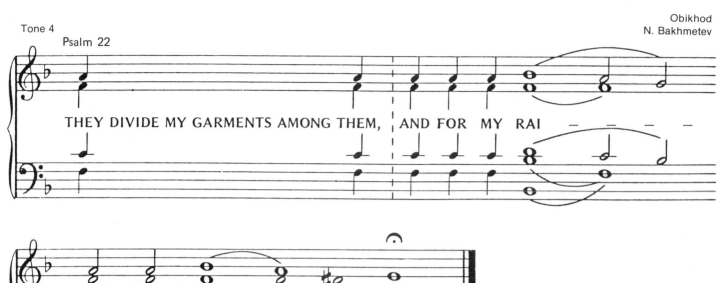

Tone 4

Psalm 22

Obikhod
N. Bakhmetev

THEY DIVIDE MY GARMENTS AMONG THEM, AND FOR MY RAI — — — —

-MENT THEY CAST LOTS.

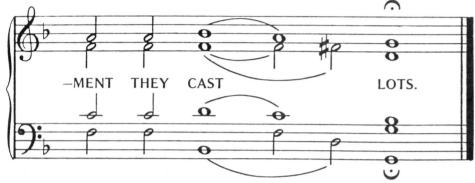

Verse: MY GOD, MY GOD, LOOK UPON ME! WHY HAST THOU FORSAKEN ME?

The First Prokeimenon

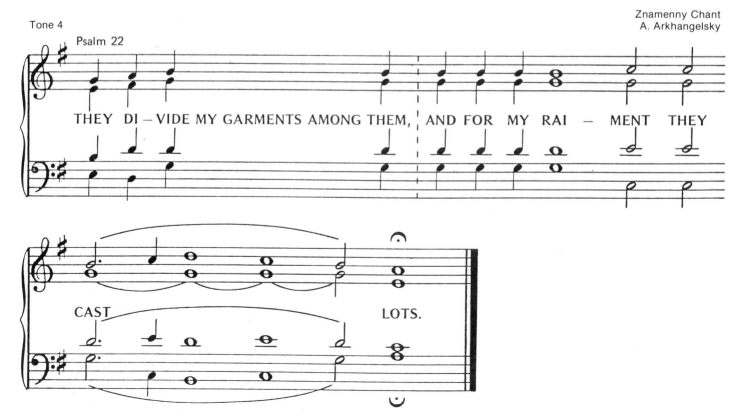

Tone 4

Psalm 22

Znamenny Chant
A. Arkhangelsky

THEY DI — VIDE MY GARMENTS AMONG THEM, AND FOR MY RAI — MENT THEY

CAST LOTS.

Verse: MY GOD, MY GOD, LOOK UPON ME! WHY HAST THOU FORSAKEN ME?

The Second Prokeimenon

Tone 4

Obikhod
N. Bakhmetev

Psalm 35

JUDGE, O LORD, THOSE WHO WRONG ME; FIGHT AGAINST THOSE WHO FIGHT A – GAINST ME.

Verse: THEY REWARDED ME EVIL FOR GOOD; MY SOUL IS FORLORN.

The Second Prokeimenon

Tone 4

Znamenny Chant
A. Arkhangelsky

Psalm 35

JUDGE, O LORD, THOSE WHO WRONG ME; FIGHT AGAINST THOSE WHO FIGHT A – GAINST ME.

Verse: THEY REWARDED ME EVIL FOR GOOD; MY SOUL IS FORLORN.

The Third Prokeimenon

Obikhod
N. Bakhmetev

Tone 6

Psalm 88

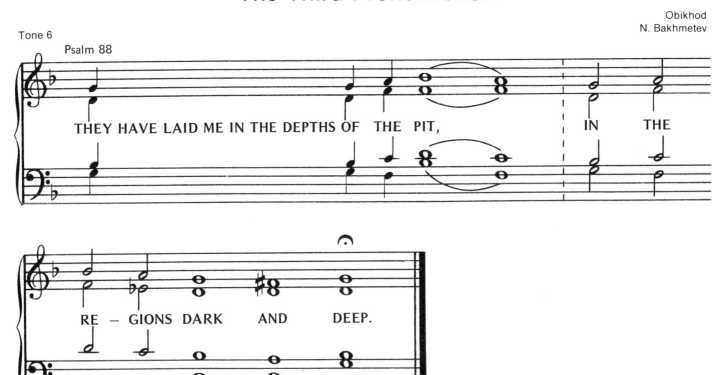

THEY HAVE LAID ME IN THE DEPTHS OF THE PIT, IN THE

RE – GIONS DARK AND DEEP.

Verse: O LORD GOD OF MY SALVATION, I CALL FOR HELP BY DAY; I CRY OUT IN THE NIGHT BEFORE THEE.

The Third Prokeimenon

Znamenny Chant
A. Arkhangelsky

Tone 6

Psalm 88

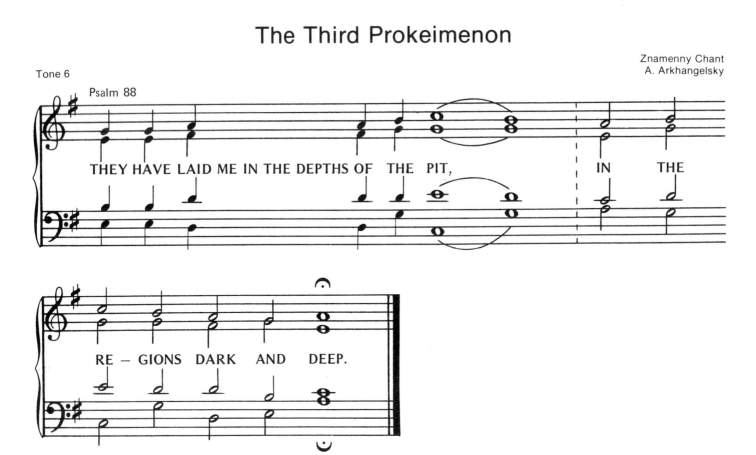

THEY HAVE LAID ME IN THE DEPTHS OF THE PIT, IN THE

RE – GIONS DARK AND DEEP.

Verse: O LORD GOD OF MY SALVATION, I CALL FOR HELP BY DAY; I CRY OUT IN THE NIGHT BEFORE THEE.

Alleluia Before the Gospel

Tone 1

Znamenny Chant
A. Arkhangelsky

Verse: SAVE ME, O GOD, FOR THE WATERS HAVE COME UP TO MY NECK.

Verse: THEY GAVE ME GALL FOR FOOD, AND IN MY THIRST THEY GAVE ME VINEGAR TO DRINK.

Verse: LET THEIR EYES BE DARKENED, SO THAT THEY CANNOT SEE.

Alleluia Before the Gospel

Modern Greek

Verses: (cf. above)

Alleluia Before the Gospel

Abbreviated Kievan Chant

Verses: (cf. above)

At the Gospel

Obikhod
N. Bakhmetev

At the Gospel

Byzantine Chant

Priest: That we may be accounted worthy...

LORD, HAVE MER—CY. LORD, HAVE MER—CY. LORD, HAVE MER — CY.

Priest: Wisdom!...Peace be unto all!

AND TO YOUR SPIR — IT.

Before the Gospel:

GLO—RY TO THY PAS — SION, O LORD.

After the Gospel:

GLO—RY TO THY LONG- SUF—FER—ING, O LORD.

At the Gospel

Priest: That we may be accounted worthy...

Russian Chant

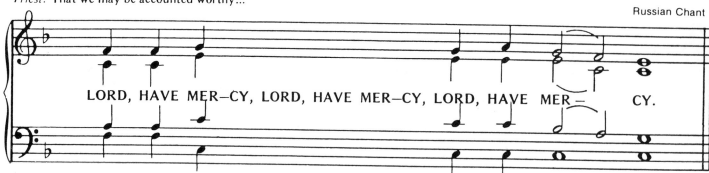

LORD, HAVE MER—CY, LORD, HAVE MER—CY, LORD, HAVE MER— CY.

Priest: Wisdom!...Peace be unto all!

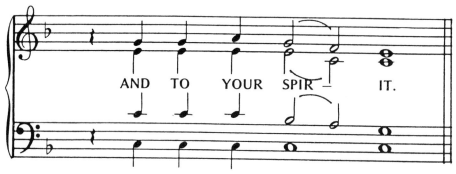

AND TO YOUR SPIR— IT.

Before the Gospel:

GLO—RY TO THY PAS—SION, O LORD.

After the Gospel:

GLO—RY TO THY LONG—SUF—FER—ING O LORD.

The Augmented Litany

Kievan Chant
B. Ledkovsky

The Augmented Litany

S. Glagolev

LORD, HAVE MER—CY. LORD, HAVE MER—CY. LORD, HAVE MERCY. LORD, HAVE

MERCY. LORD, HAVE MER—CY. LORD, HAVE MERCY. LORD, HAVE MERCY. LORD

HAVE MER—CY. A—MEN.

The Augmented Litany

Znamenny Chant
A. Arkhangelsky

The Augmented Litany

Russian Chant

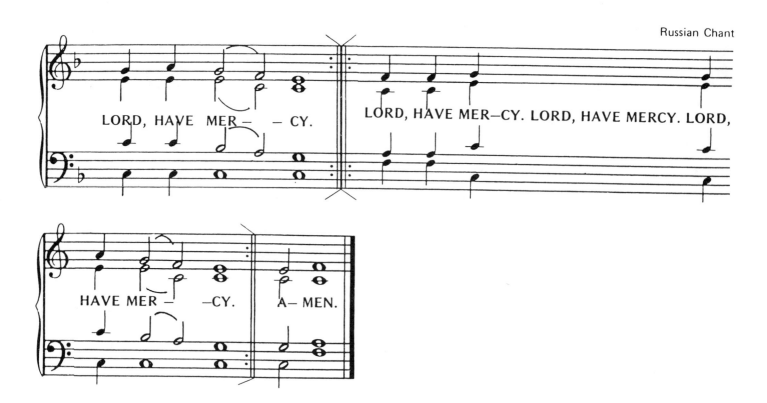

Vouchsafe, O Lord

Vouchsafe, O Lord, to keep us this night without sin.
Blessed art Thou, O Lord God of our fathers, and praise and glorified be Thy name forever.
Amen.

Let Thy mercy, O Lord, be upon us, as we have set our hope on Thee.
Blessed art Thou, O Lord; teach me Thy statutes!
Blessed art Thou, O Master; make me to understand Thy commandments!
Blessed art Thou, O Holy One; enlighten me with Thy precepts!

Thy mercy, O Lord, endureth forever; O despise not the works of Thy hands!
To Thee belongeth worship, to Thee belongeth praise, to Thee belongeth glory:
to the Father, and to the Son, and to the Holy Spirit, now and ever and unto ages of ages.
Amen.

The Litany of Fervent Supplication

Kievan Chant
B. Ledkovsky

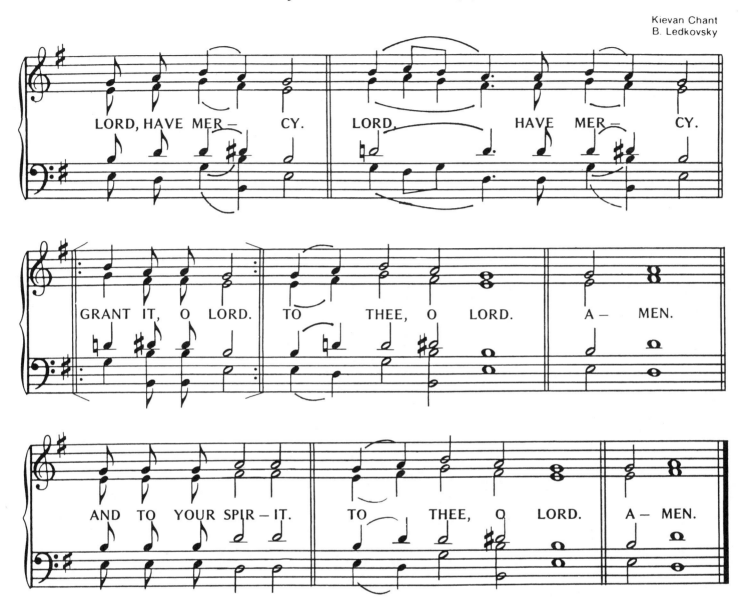

The Litany of Fervent Supplication

Russian Chant

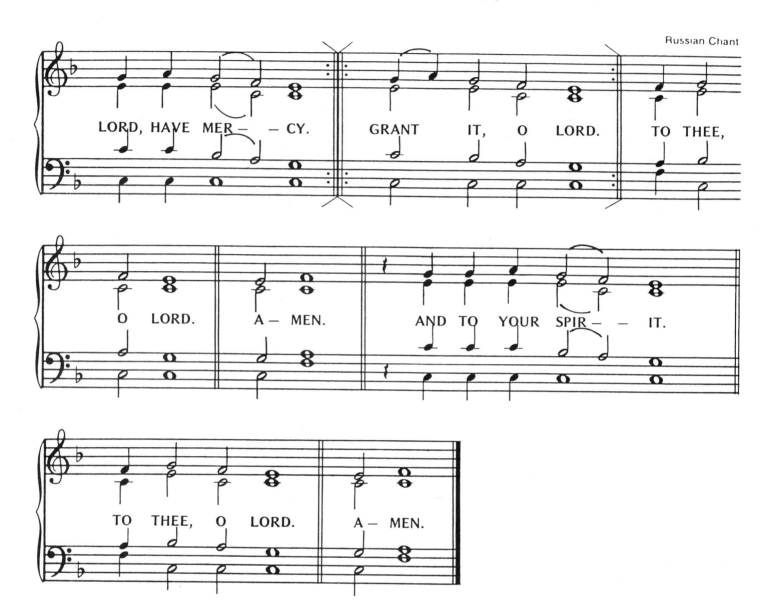

LORD, HAVE MER — — CY.   GRANT IT, O LORD.   TO THEE,

O LORD.   A — MEN.   AND TO YOUR SPIR — — IT.

TO THEE, O LORD.   A — MEN.

The Litany of Fervent Supplication

Znamenny Chant
A. Arkhangelsky

The Apostikha

Obikhod
N. Bakhmetev

Tone 2

JOS—EPH OF AR—I—MA—THE—A TOOK THEE DOWN FROM THE TREE, THE LIFE OF ALL, COLD IN DEATH. BATH — ING THEE WITH SWEET AND COST — LY MYRRH, HE GENTLY COVERED THEE WITH FIN—EST LIN — EN AND WITH SOR—ROW AND TEN—DER LOVE IN HIS HEART HE EM—BRACED THY MOST PURE BOD — Y. TREM—BLING AT THIS AWE — SOME SIGHT HE CRIED

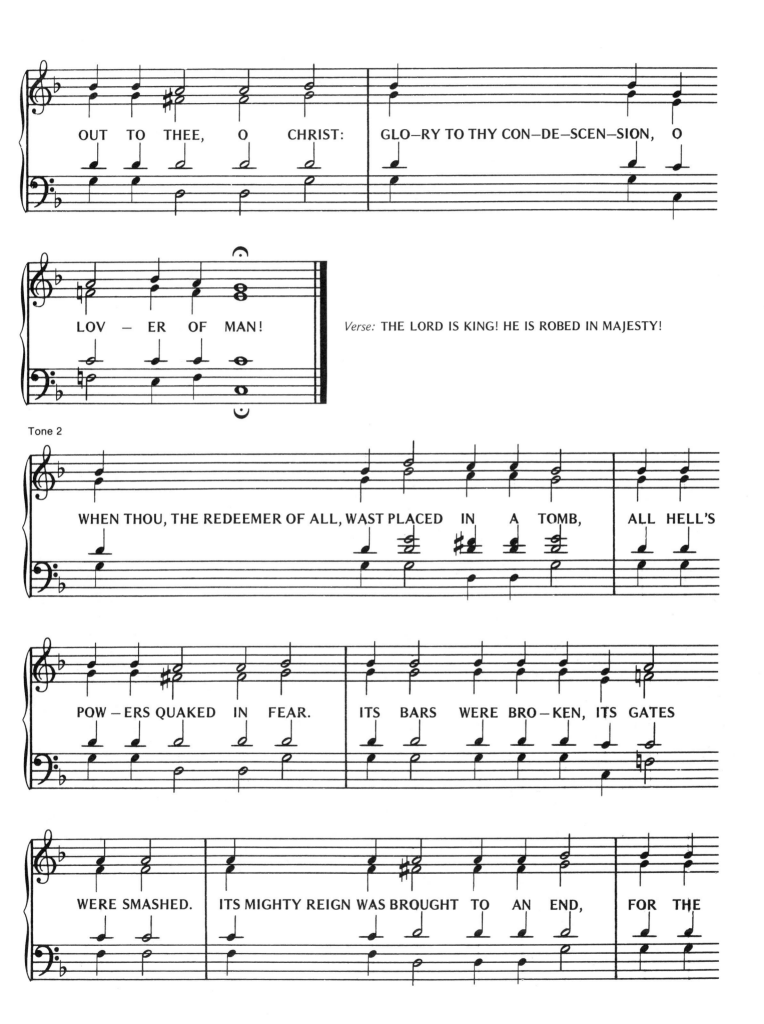

DEAD CAME FORTH A – LIVE FROM THEIR TOMBS, CAST – ING OFF THE BONDS OF

THEIR CAP – TIV – I – TY. AD – AM WAS FILLED WITH JOY!

HE GRATEFULLY CRIED OUT TO THEE, O CHRIST: GLO – RY TO THY CON – DE –

–SCEN–SION, O LOV – ER OF MAN!

Verse: HE HAS ESTABLISHED THE WORLD
SO THAT IT SHALL NEVER BE MOVED.

Tone 2

IN THE FLESH THOU WAST WILLINGLY EN–CLOSED IN THE TOMB, WHO ART

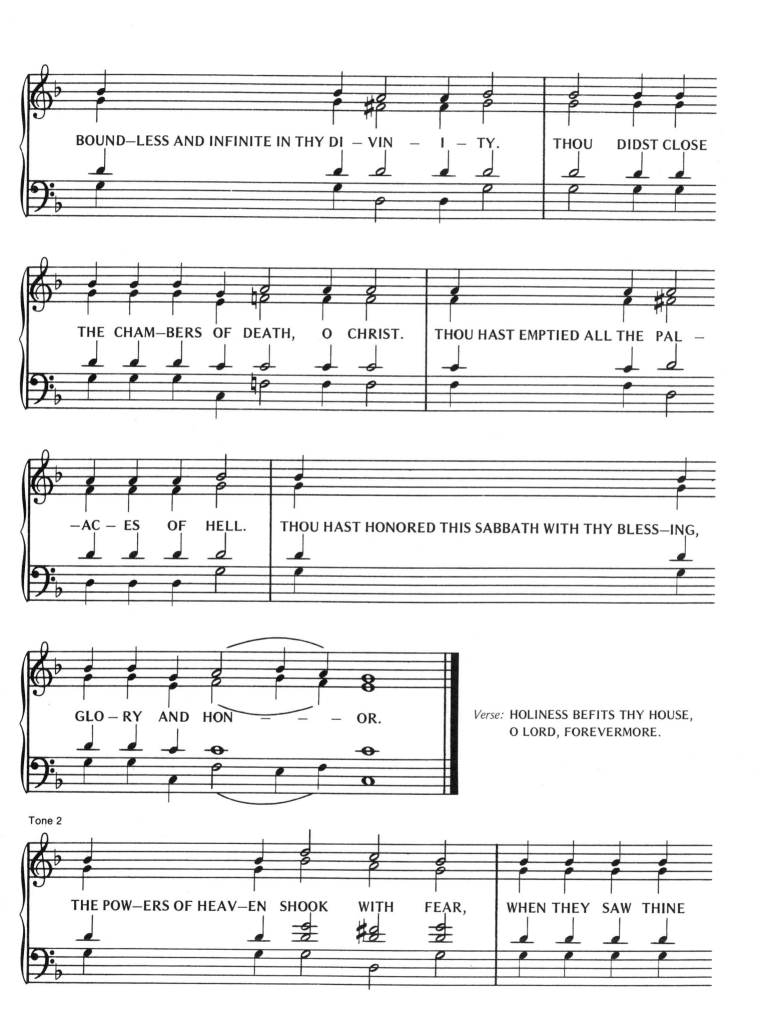

BOUND—LESS AND INFINITE IN THY DI — VIN — I — TY. THOU DIDST CLOSE

THE CHAM—BERS OF DEATH, O CHRIST. THOU HAST EMPTIED ALL THE PAL —

—AC — ES OF HELL. THOU HAST HONORED THIS SABBATH WITH THY BLESS—ING,

GLO — RY AND HON — — — OR.

Verse: HOLINESS BEFITS THY HOUSE, O LORD, FOREVERMORE.

Tone 2

THE POW—ERS OF HEAV—EN SHOOK WITH FEAR, WHEN THEY SAW THINE

GLO—RY TO THY CON—DE—SCEN—SION, O LOV — ER OF MAN!

Verse: GLORY TO THE FATHER, AND TO THE SON, AND TO THE HOLY SPIRIT,
NOW AND EVER, AND UNTO AGES OF AGES. AMEN.

Tone 5

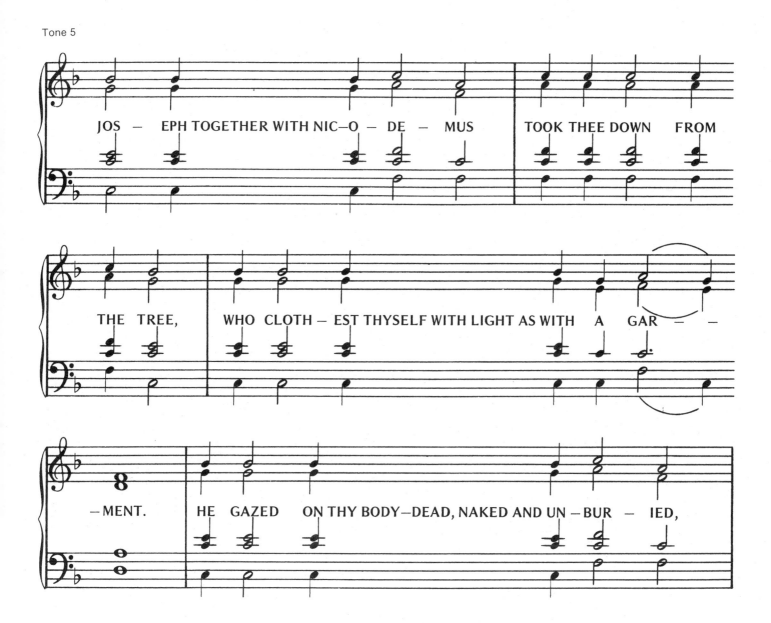

JOS — EPH TOGETHER WITH NIC—O—DE — MUS   TOOK THEE DOWN   FROM

THE TREE,   WHO CLOTH — EST THYSELF WITH LIGHT AS WITH   A   GAR — —

—MENT.   HE GAZED   ON THY BODY—DEAD, NAKED AND UN —BUR — IED,

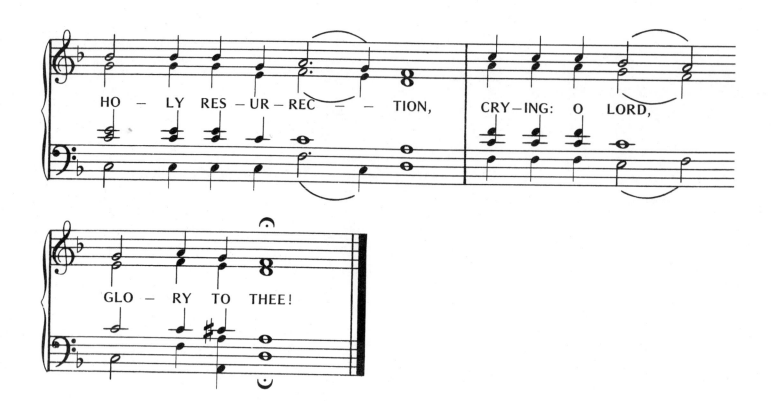

HO — LY RES — UR — REC — — TION, CRY—ING: O LORD,

GLO — RY TO THEE!

The Apostikha

Tone 2

Optino Monastery Chant
Special Melody (Samopodoben)

JOS—EPH OF AR—I—MA—THE—A TOOK THEE DOWN FROM THE TREE, THE LIFE OF ALL, COLD IN DEATH. BATH—ING THEE WITH SWEET AND COST — — LY MYRRH, HE GENTLY COVERED THEE WITH FIN—EST LIN — — EN AND WITH SOR—ROW AND TEN—DER LOVE IN HIS HEART HE EMBRACED THY MOST PURE BOD — —Y. TREM—BLING AT THIS AWE — — SOME SIGHT HE CRIED OUT TO

THEE, O CHRIST: GLO—RY TO THY CON—DE—SCEN—SION, O LOV—ER OF MAN!

8

Verse: THE LORD IS KING! HE IS ROBED IN MAJESTY!

Tone 2

WHEN THOU, THE RE—DEEM—ER OF ALL, WAST PLACED IN A TOMB, ALL HELL'S

POW—ERS QUAKED IN FEAR. ITS BARS WERE BROKEN, ITS GATES WERE

SMASHED! ITS MIGHT—Y REIGN WAS BROUGHT TO AN END, FOR THE DEAD

CAME FORTH A—LIVE FROM THEIR TOMBS, CAST—ING OFF THE BONDS OF THEIR

CAP—TIV — I — TY. AD—AM WAS FILLED WITH JOY! HE GRATE—FUL—LY

CRIED OUT TO THEE, O CHRIST: GLO—RY TO THY CON—DE—SCEN—SION, O

LOV — ER OF MAN!

Verse: HE HAS ESTABLISHED THE WORLD SO THAT IT SHALL NEVER BE MOVED.

Tone 2

IN THE FLESH THOU WAST WILL—ING—LY EN—CLOSED IN THE TOMB, WHO ART

BOUND—LESS AND INFINITE IN THY DI — VIN — I — TY. THOU DIDST CLOSE THE

CHAM—BERS OF DEATH, O CHRIST. THOU HAST EMPTIED ALL THE PAL—AC—ES

OF HELL. THOU HAST HONORED THIS SABBATH WITH THY BLESSING, GLO—RY

AND HON — — OR.

Verse: HOLINESS BEFITS THY HOUSE, O LORD, FOREVERMORE.

Tone 2

THE POW—ERS OF HEAV—EN SHOOK WITH FEAR, WHEN THEY SAW THINE

IN—EF—FA—BLE FOR—BEAR — — ANCE. THEY BEHELD THEE SLANDERED BY

Verse: GLORY TO THE FATHER, AND TO THE SON, AND TO THE HOLY SPIRIT,
NOW AND EVER, AND UNTO AGES OF AGES. AMEN.

Pskov Melody
H. Benigsen

Tone 5

JOS—EPH TO-GETH-ER WITH NIC—O—DE———MUS TOOK THEE DOWN

FROM THE TREE, WHO CLOTH—EST THYSELF WITH LIGHT AS WITH A GAR———

MENT. HE GAZED ON THY BODY, DEAD, NA—KED AND UN—BUR———IED,

AND IN GRIEF AND TENDER COMPASSION HE LA—MENT—ED: WOE IS ME,

MY SWEET—EST JE———SUS! A SHORT WHILE A—GO, THE SUN

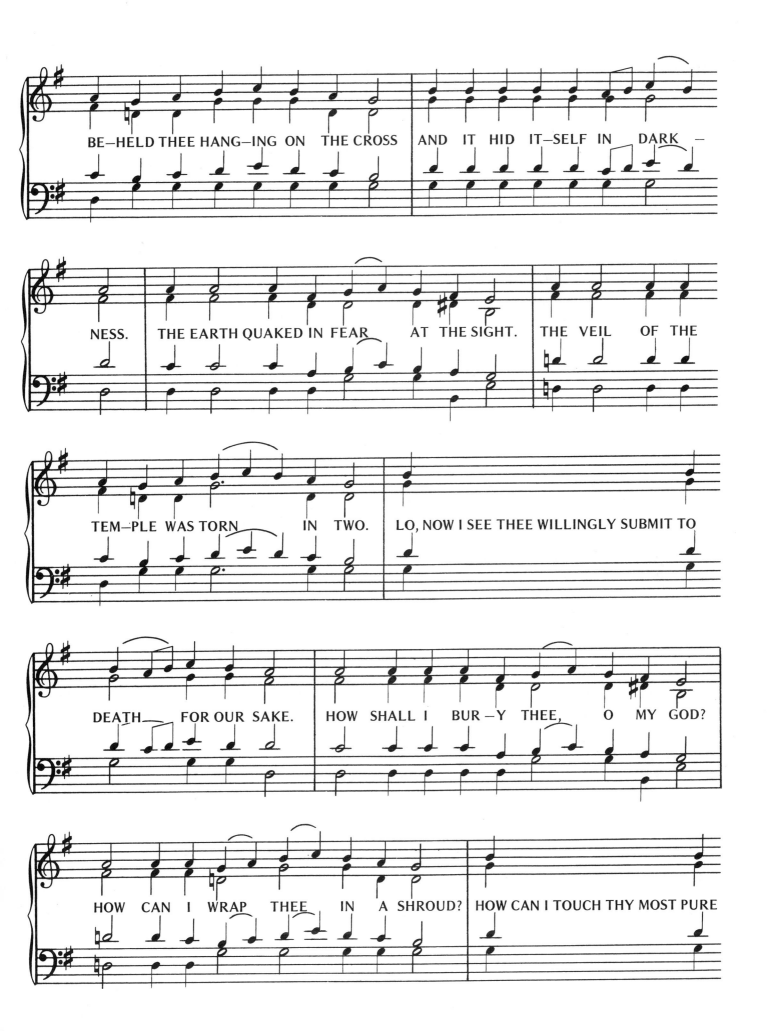

The Prayer of St. Simeon

READER:

Lord, now lettest Thou Thy servant depart in peace, according to Thy word,
for mine eyes have seen Thy salvation,
which Thou hast prepared before the face of all peoples:
a light to enlighten the Gentiles,
and to be the glory of Thy people Israel.

The Trisagion Prayers

Holy God, Holy Mighty, Holy Immortal, have mercy on us!
Holy God, Holy Mighty, Holy Immortal, have mercy on us!
Holy God, Holy Mighty, Holy Immortal, have mercy on us!

Glory to the Father, and to the Son, and to the Holy Spirit, now and ever, and unto ages of ages. Amen.

O Most-Holy Trinity, have mercy on us!

O Lord, cleanse us from our sins!

O Master, pardon our transgressions!

O Holy One, visit and heal our infirmities, for Thy Name's sake.

Lord, have mercy. Lord, have mercy. Lord, have mercy.

Glory to the Father, and to the Son, and to the Holy Spirit, now and ever, and unto ages of ages. Amen.

Our Father, who art in heaven, hallowed be Thy Name!
Thy Kingdom come! Thy will be done, on earth as it is in heaven.
Give us this day our daily bread, and forgive us our trespasses, as we forgive those who trespass against us;
and lead us not into temptation, but deliver us from evil.

The Noble Joseph

Bulgarian Melody

THE NO — — BLE JOS — — EPH WHEN HE HAD TAK — EN DOWN THY MOST PURE BOD — — Y FROM THE TREE WRAPPED IT IN

271

FINE LIN — — EN AND A — NOINT

— ED IT WITH SPIC — ES AND

PLACED IT IN A NEW TOMB.

(cf. p. 272 for Alternate "Glory....")

GLO — RY TO THE FA — — THER AND TO THE

SON AND TO THE HO — LY SPIR — — — — IT,

NOW AND EV — ER AND UN — — TO A — —

—GES OF A — — GES. A — — MEN.

(cf. next page for "The angel..."

Alternate "Glory...."

GLO — RY TO THE FA — — THER AND TO THE

SON AND TO THE HO —LY SPIR — — IT,

NOW AND EV — ER AND UN — — TO A — —

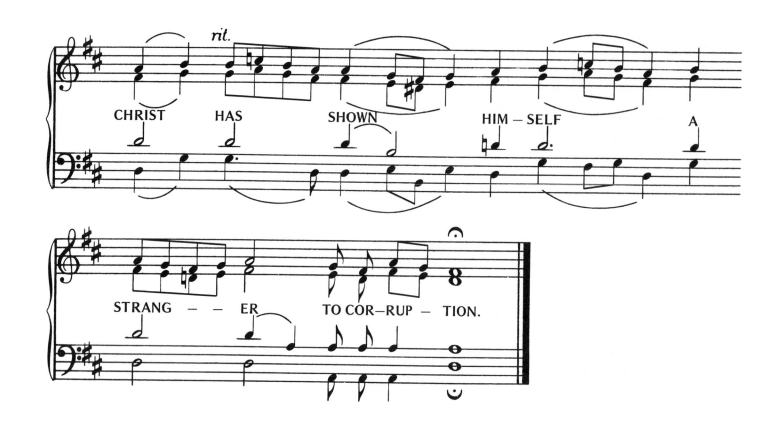

CHRIST HAS SHOWN HIM—SELF A STRANG — — ER TO COR—RUP — TION.

The Noble Joseph

Greek Melody

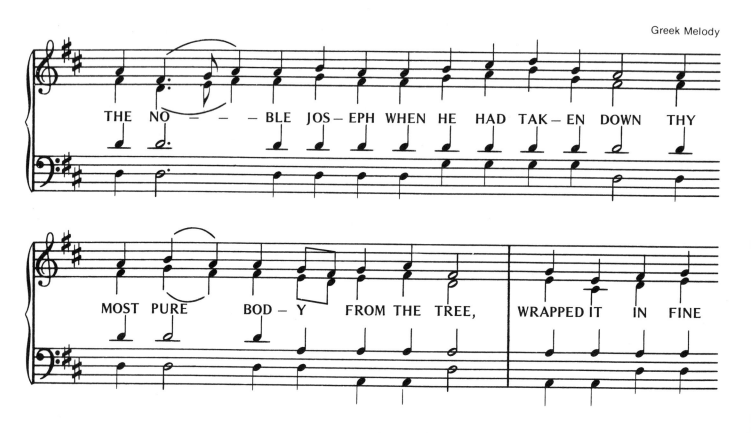

THE NO — — BLE JOS—EPH WHEN HE HAD TAK—EN DOWN THY MOST PURE BOD—Y FROM THE TREE, WRAPPED IT IN FINE

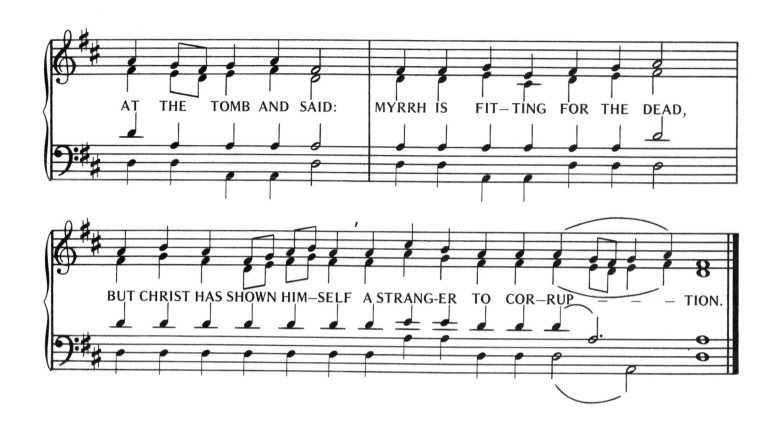

The Noble Joseph

Serbian Melody

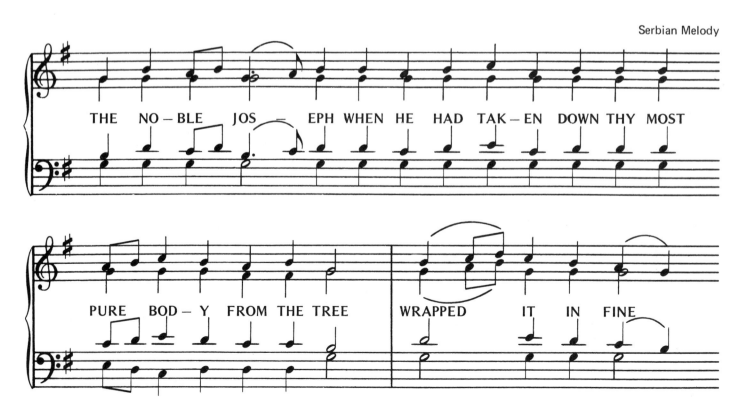

LIN — — — EN AND A—NOINT—ED IT WITH SPIC — — —

— ES AND PLACED IT IN A NEW TOMB.

GLO—RY TO THE FA — THER AND TO THE SON AND TO

THE HO — LY SPIR — IT.

NOW AND EV — ER AND UNTO A—GES OF A — GES. A — MEN.

278

The Great Dismissal

280

Come, Let Us Bless Joseph

Tone 5

Pskov Chant
H. Benigsen

TEM—PLE NOW HAS COME TO PASS: A SWORD HAS PIERCED

MY HEART; BUT CHANGE MY GRIEF TO GLADNESS BY THY RES—UR—

—REC — — TION.'" WE WOR — SHIP THY PAS—SION, O

CHRIST! WE WORSHIP THY PAS—SION, O CHRIST! WE WOR—SHIP THY

PAS—SION, O CHRIST, AND THY HO—LY RES—UR—REC — TION!

Come, Let Us Bless Joseph

D. Bortniansky

286

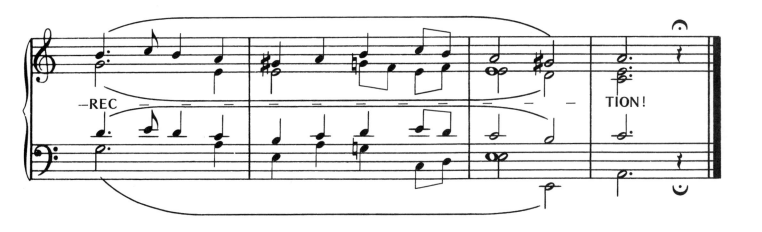